Airborne Equipment

Airborne Equipment

A History of its Development

John Weeks

HIPPOCRENE
BOOKS, INC.

New York, N. Y.

By the same author **Men Against Tanks**

Library of Congress Catalog Card Number 76–487
ISBN 0–88254–401–2

Printed in Great Britain

Contents

Introduction

There have been so many books about airborne warfare and parachute operations that the reader may be wondering why yet another should be written. The battles and raids of World War II and the post-war operations in different parts of the world have been described, examined, dissected and explained in the minutest detail by a small army of competent and expert authors. The names of the major battles are almost household words, their anniversaries are celebrated each year, and the veterans parade by their war memorials. It is recent history and the participants are still with us.

But there is one aspect of this history that has not so far been examined in any detail and it is usually not mentioned in the official histories except in passing: this aspect is the equipment of the airborne soldier, his weapons, his parachute, his aeroplane, and his glider. This book is devoted to that subject.

Airborne soldiers are like armoured soldiers: their battle is shaped by their equipment. With a poor tank and an inadequate gun an armoured force is at an immediate disadvantage, and no matter how brave and resourceful they may be, in a straight fight they are bound to come out the loser. The tank battles of the Western Desert confirm this. Only by some remarkable predominance in tactics, or by taking advantage of dangerous weaknesses in the mentality of the enemy can the poorly equipped force hope to gain a victory. The Israelis have been the post-war experts in the exploitation of the feebleness of their opponent, but such a disparity of competence as presently exists between them and the Egyptians is most unusual, and it may not last.

In airborne warfare, to launch a force into a parachute landing with insufficient heavy weapons, or too few anti-tank guns, or too little fighter cover – or some other equally important shortcoming – is to invite disaster. For the airborne force fights its battle on its own; if things become too hot for it there is no withdrawal, no quiet fading away behind the comfortable barrier of another divisional front, and no retiring behind a screen of artillery fire. It is literally 'Win or Bust', and all too often it has been 'Bust' rather than 'Win'. Everything is staked on the first throw of the dice. If that goes wrong, all goes wrong. There is so little room for manoeuvre.

This book sets out therefore to examine the tools of the airborne soldier's trade, what it was that he used in the land battle, how he got to the battle, and why he did it in that way. Inevitably the major portion of the book concentrates on World War II, for that war introduced the concept of airborne war in a most dramatic manner and it brought it to a rapid crescendo in a series of spectacular and impressive battles. We shall never see the like of those battles again, for modern anti-aircraft missiles and radar systems make it impossible for any country to launch such huge air armadas with any hope of success. Nor could a modern airforce contemplate the losses in men and material that they would suffer in the resupply and support of a major airborne battle deep in enemy territory. The scene has changed and it is as well to pick out and record the detail in the past picture before it fades. Nowadays the emphasis is more upon short raids, quick 'seize and hold' operations upon objectives a short distance from the main force, or a reinforcement, or a coup d'état. The equipment of the 1940s demanded a massive effort in men and machines to launch the airborne attacks, and a similar effort to sustain them. There is something awesome in contemplating the gigantic preparations which preceded the Arnhem and Rhine operations, the intricate and precise timing, the linking up of different elements and the incredible bravery of the men who carried it through. These were huge and ponderous military adventures whose form and timing was forced upon them by the equipment that was available.

There is no more obvious example of the changes in the post-war airborne scene than that brought about by the introduction of the large transport aeroplane with its rear-loading doors and skid-board method of parachuting heavy loads. The first one of these machines killed the glider for the carriage of equipment in airborne operations, and one of the marvels of this story is the rapid speed of the introduction of cargo gliders and their equally rapid departure from the inventory. It is a history that takes little more than seven years from the start of the first models to the disappearance of all but a very few. In that time huge fleets of these machines were built, sometimes in wood by makers of domestic furniture, often in steel; mile upon mile of special rope was made to tow them; hundreds of bombing aircraft were diverted from their proper tasks to pull them; thousands of men were allocated to maintain them and marshal them on their airfields. Specially trained pilots were recruited – and all for what? To carry the vital heavy equipment to an airborne battle, a one-way trip for almost every glider. The cost and complexity of the whole thing is staggering. Nowadays the same equipment can be loaded into a transport aeroplane, flown at 400mph or 500mph and parachuted accurately and quickly onto a drop zone many hundreds of miles from the plane's home base. The cycle can be repeated as often as required, all other circumstances permitting, and the manpower required to achieve it is a fraction of what the same 'lift' of gliders would need.

This book does not set out to relate the accounts of the battles and their effects upon the war. The reader must turn to others for that information. The bibliography lists a number of reliable sources, the best of which is undoubtedly Maurice Tugwell's *Airborne to Battle*. Colonel Tugwell traces the history of airborne warfare in detail from the earliest endeavours and any reader unfamiliar with the background will find it a useful guide to have by when reading this book.

The sources for a work of this kind are inevitably varied, but in every case where a particular equipment is mentioned care has been taken to check the detail either with a surviving example, or with official documents such as training manuals, or from the recollections of survivors. Some of the photographs have been published before and are shown again because there are no others to portray a particular facet; other photographs have not been seen in public before, and I am deeply grateful to those who helped me to find them and gave me permission to use them.

1 Parachutes

The general history of parachuting is long but scantily record-ed. The history of military parachuting on the other hand is short and almost embarrassingly well documented. The former extends over 200 years, the latter over four decades. The same principles hold good for each, and this chapter con-fines itself to a brief study of the basic tool of the parachute soldier, his parachute itself.

Early days

Most of the early parachutes were operated by the parachutist falling away from his aircraft and pulling out the parachute – in other words, some general method of static-line operation. Throughout the nineteenth century, acrobats and gymnasts were lifted up by balloons at fairs and similar outdoor shows and then floated down on some form of parachute to the de-light and wonderment of the crowd. These were simple designs, often barely packed at all, but carried below a balloon basket spread out and held by thin cords which broke under the weight of the parachutist as he fell free. Opening was assured, and the number of recorded accidents is remarkably few. In World War I, when observation balloons were being shot down by fighter aircraft, the idea was revived and obser-vers were given a parachute stowed in an aluminium sleeve on the outside of the basket. A single rope led out from this sleeve, which the observer hitched to a primitive harness and, when the dangers of remaining overcame his fears of leaving, he jumped and pulled out the canopy after him. These 'Guardian Angels', as the commercial name went, were reliable and safe. They were used frequently during the war for saving the lives of balloon observers, and afterwards were adapted to aero-planes as emergency equipment. Subsequently they were over-shadowed by the manually operated 'chute developed by Leslie Irvin, but the idea was well proven, and remained in the minds of some military thinkers.

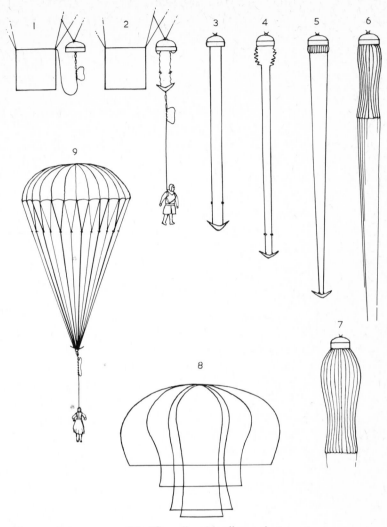

The opening sequence of the 'Guardian Angel' parachute.

  1 The parachute hanging on the side of a balloon basket.

  2 Jumping out.

3–6 The deployment of the rigging lines, followed by the canopy.

7–8 The canopy opening, 8 shows the way in which it fills out from the top downwards.

  9 The parachute fully developed.

This opening sequence was used in a modified form on the X-type of 1941 and is typical of all 'canopy last' parachutes.

The Italian example

When Italy began to experiment with parachute troops in 1927 they used their existing aircrew life-saver – the 'Salvatore' which was a development of the Guardian Angel but it had the parachute on the back of the man rather than attached to the plane, and the static line which opened it was also on the man and simply had to be attached to a strong point before jumping. The system has only varied in detail to this very day. The Salvatore was reliable and quick in opening, both virtues required of a military parachute, and it allowed men to be dropped at low altitudes without danger. In fact the opening was almost too quick since the canopy was hardly out of the slipstream before it was fully developed, and it must have exerted a considerable shock on the man as it snapped open. The harness was simple to the point of being primitive, for it was little more than a broad canvas belt with shoulder and leg straps. The rigging lines led to a single suspension point at the back of the belt and this must have meant that the opening of the canopy was something that one really remembered, since the full weight of the body would be taken on the solar plexus. After this unpleasant beginning the remaining flight was hardly more comfortable since the jumper hung slightly face forwards from his one suspension point, sometimes gently rotating, and he had to land in this position. The Irvin harness was already known at the time the Salvatore was being made, and it is a mystery why the Italians never adopted it. Italy continued to experiment with this type of 'chute until the beginning of World War II, but it was never used in action, nor in great numbers for training.

Russia

The Italian developments may or may not have inspired the next appearance of the military parachute when in 1930 the Soviet Union started work upon what was later to become its famous and feared airborne army. During the manoeuvres of that year a force of nine men was dropped by parachute with complete success, and from this small beginning were built up the large airborne forces of later years.

In 1931, 600 descents were made by Russian aviators, and in

An early Soviet method of exit. Pre-war Russian parachutists sliding off the wing of an ANT-6 and rolling off into space. (*Imperial War Museum*)

1932 more than 2,000 were made by military personnel. By 1935, there were 1,300 parachute clubs in the Soviet Union, 115 parachute centres, 370 training towers and more than 8,000 civilian men and women under training. By 1936 a battalion was dropped, and the next year it was a regiment. In both cases the jumping was filmed and photographed so that the techniques used can be studied today. Intriguingly, the Russians had followed a different path from the Italians, and had adopted a copy of the Irvin flat circular canopy, manually operated by a ripcord, using no static lines. This promptly imposed three highly undesirable limitations. Firstly the jumping height had to be greater than with the Salvatore, and secondly the exit from the plane had to be performed with much more care. Finally the training of the man took longer and was more expensive. However, the Russians overcame these difficulties although they soon abandoned the ripcord process after 1936 and turned to the more normal static line.

A 1935 film shows one 'stick' leaving their ANT-6 monoplane. The ANT-6 was a very large four-engined mid-winged plane, which could fly at a very slow speed without stalling. In the film the stick is controlled by a man whom we should now call a 'jumpmaster' who stood up in a forward cockpit or hatch and faced aft. The parachutists climbed out and lowered themselves onto the broad wing from another hatch. Here they held on to handles and watched the jumpmaster who signalled to them to let go by waving a small flag. The parachutists then slid down the wing and pulled their ripcords just as they cleared the trailing edge. It is an extraordinary way of managing a military jump, and it would never have worked at all but for the incredibly low flying speed of the ANT-6 which must have been somewhere close to 60mph. Even so, the sticks must have been spread out over a long distance on the drop zone. These men carried no weapons or visible equipment, and presumably all their equipment came down in bundles dropped from bomb racks under the same plane.

German initiatives

The Germans watched these Soviet experiments with interest and adapted some of the features to their own ideas. They immediately saw that the ripcord idea was of little military value, and almost from the beginning a static-line parachute was developed. This was the first of the RZ (*Rückenpackung Zwangaulösung*) series. RZ 1 was a 28ft shaped circular canopy which remained in service until replaced in early 1940. It was not particularly stable and there were complaints of excessive oscillation in flight; it also suffered from failures with the deployment of the static line, and these failures were usually fatal. The next model was the RZ 16, which was quickly followed by the RZ 20, which was the standard model from early 1941 until the end of the war. Although the inspiration for the RZ models probably came from the Italian Salvatore, the later versions had several differences. The greatest one concerned the harness. The seat strap of the Irvin was used, and the three connectors in front of the body, but the method of running the extensions of the harness up to the

A German parachutist descending with his RZ 20 canopy. The curious method of suspension causes him to hang slightly face-downward. (*Imperial War Museum*)

rigging lines was abandoned and the Salvatore single-point suspension retained. This was a mistake and the *Fallschirmjaeger* paid for it in every jump.

In flight the jumper hung from two strops, which were attached to the back of his harness, and had no way to prevent himself rotating, nor could he exercise even the most elementary control over his parachute. This, as we have seen, was one of the faults of the Salvatore. His body hung in a slightly face-downward attitude, and he was taught to swing himself round to face the direction of drift by making quick jerky 'swimming' motions with his arms and legs. A satisfactory landing could be made only in a forward direction, and was achieved by an exaggerated form of the forward roll or tumble. Thick rubber knee – and sometimes elbow – pads helped to absorb the worst of the shock.

The advantage which the German RZ parachute had over any that the Russians had used lay in the fact that from the first it was designed for static-line opening. The line itself was a length of rope which hooked to a strong point in the aeroplane with a snap hook. When the line had paid out it pulled the back pack open and jerked out the canopy in one bundle. The line then tugged the cover clear and remained attached to the plane with the empty canopy bag trailing in the slipstream alongside the fuselage. The canopy, being so sharply flung into the fast-moving airstream, opened rapidly while the rigging lines paid out as the man fell away. The result was a hard opening shock, but a very quick one, and a feature of the RZ was that the parachutists could be dropped from altitudes well below anything attempted by the Allies. The normal jumping height was between 380 and 400ft, but in action it was sometimes less than that, and one of the lifts in the Crete operation jumped without harm from 250ft.

The German parachutists were taught to pack their own 'chutes and this used to be dramatically demonstrated in a pre-war German training film which was kept at the RAF Parachute Training School until a few years ago. The film was very much a propaganda effort as well as training, and all the men who appeared on the screen were superb specimens of Aryan manhood: blonde, tall, and rippling with controlled muscle.

The film showed all aspects of jump training, including how to exit from the Junkers 52. This was no ordinary way of leaving the plane. The trainee was taught to stand in the door, bent forward with feet apart, toes on the sill, hands round each side of the door and looking outwards towards the horizon. On jumping he sprang out headfirst spreadeagling his body with legs and arms outstretched, remaining like that until his parachute opened, in a way reminiscent of the sort of exit that a modern free-fall parachutist makes from a door. To teach this rather difficult athletic manoeuvre a dummy fuselage was rigged above a large net, and the student hurled himself into this. The camera was cleverly angled to make the most of this jump, and it never failed to get an appreciative gasp from a British service audience. Other sequences dealt with the landing, and the elaborate emphasis that was placed on making satisfactory forward rolls. One saw students racing along elevated walkways and hurling themselves into the air from a height of several feet to land on mats and do a rapid tumble before leaping up and running away.

The packing sequence showed an RZ canopy being folded in much the same way as all canopies are, and being carefully stowed into its bag. The rigging lines were then drawn together into a rope and packed down on top of the canopy, as a sailor stows an anchor chain. Finally, the last few metres were quickly drawn off the table and coiled on top of the remainder and the whole bag tied up with light cord. Such a packing method is perfectly satisfactory, although it always leaves the suspicion that it can lead to accidents. Allied packing drills were infinitely stricter and great care was, and still is, taken to ensure that rigging lines are carefully stowed in elastic pockets to ensure that they pay out in a straight line without tangling.

The result of the RZ design was that the German parachutist had to be a fit and agile man. Furthermore, that particular parachute was not at all well suited to occasional use by persons not specifically trained to it, and in this respect it was inferior to the Allied types which were often given to agents and similar clandestine operators who jumped with them quite safely after only minimal training. Indeed, in one of the postwar jumps into Greece a Greek general of advanced age landed

17

perfectly safely from his first and only jump with a British X-type having had no training whatever. There is little doubt that had he done that with a RZ he would have been remarkably lucky not to have been badly injured.

The RZ parachute was typical of so many other items of German equipment in World War II. When it was produced in the middle 1930s it was a great innovation, and large numbers were made. But in order to mass produce these large numbers the design had to be fixed, and by the time it came to be used in the war it was already obsolescent, and rapidly became obsolete in the face of advancing technology on the Allied side. Probably its greatest drawback was that a parachutist using the RZ could not carry any offensive equipment beyond a sub machine-gun stuck into his lift webs, thus all his normal weapons, radios, and ammunition had to be dropped in containers. This system imposed long delays on the drop zone while the right containers were found and unpacked, and it is an established fact that the German rallying procedure took longer than did that of the Allies.

Russian developments

The Russians had advanced to some extent in the years between 1936 and 1940, and they were still a formidable parachute army, but they had not really grasped the supreme advantage of airborne forces – their strategic mobility over long distances – and too little attention had been paid to providing a fleet of suitable transport aircraft. The aged ANT-6 was still being used in 1940 when it was well out of date and until some Lease-Lend C-47s arrived three years later there was nothing to replace it except a few elderly bombers. The result of this partial neglect was that not much effort was put into developing other items of airborne equipment. Only one made any progress, and this was the personal parachute, a fundamental item.

There was a square parachute in Russia before the war, and its performance obviously encouraged the Soviets to change

The German method of exit from the Ju-52. The static line has just tightened and will pull out the canopy within the next fraction of a second. The next man to jump is hunched in the door. (*Imperial War Museum*)

over to it from their modified Irvins. They did this during the last years of the 1930s and by 1940 all Soviet jumpers had a square 'chute. So incidentally did many aircrews. The square canopy has some advantages over the circular, the chief one being that it flies very steadily without swinging or oscillating. On the other hand it cannot easily be manoeuvred or steered. The author knows only one man who has jumped with one of these wartime Russian parachutes, and he reported that it was a remarkably smooth ride and once he realised that it was useless to try to direct his flight he simply enjoyed himself and came in to a soft and straight landing. However, it was slow to open, although this meant that when it did there was little shock. But slow opening parachutes need more height to ensure each man is supported by a fully developed canopy before he lands, and the Soviet dropping height was above that used by the Western Allies, generally being between 1,000 and 1,300ft.

These Russian square canopies were mostly silk or rayon as nylon took a long time to reach Russia. They were bulky and heavy compared to nylon, and more care was needed in maintaining them. A square canopy is in any case more bulky than a similar area of circular canopy when both are packed – another of the inherent drawbacks to the square – but it does have the great advantage that it is easier and cheaper to make. Soviet square canopies were made by sewing strips of material together along their length, and crossing the completed square with tapes at right angles to the strips and diagonally. The rigging lines were led over in tunnels sewn into the material in the same manner as with round canopies. However, some Russian cargo 'chutes took only the rigging lines as far as the peripheral hem, where they were sewn firmly. Whether this system was ever used for man-carrying canopies is not at all clear.

By leaving out two rigging lines in the hem at the back of the parachutists, a larger 'lobe' was formed in the canopy, and the air underneath could escape in the form of a very low-pressure jet facing backwards. The reaction to this jet was to give the canopy a slow forward motion thus ensuring that in most weather conditions the parachutist would land in a forward direction which is the easiest to accept and the least likely to

20

injure him. It was neat and simple and all present-day sky-divers use highly sophisticated versions of it to guide themselves to their targets. However, should the jumper be so unfortunate, or so unwise, as to turn himself so that he faces downwind, then of course he lands at a greater speed than he would with a plain circular canopy, and in parachute landings speed means injuries. So the advantages of the square were not always so clear cut as they seemed at first sight.

Another peculiarity of the Russian pre-war parachuting techniques was that both main and reserve canopies were often opened. Quite why they should have done this is not now clear. It must be agreed that two canopies reduce oscillation to practically nothing, but they also reduce any form of control to practically nothing and the parachutist is left to land pretty well as the wind blows him. The reserve parachute does tend to fly downwind, which helps to make for a forward landing, but it can often be a fast forward landing and, lest any reader should imagine that two parachutes descend twice as slowly as one, he can be assured that it doesn't happen that way at all. The difference in vertical speed is barely noticeable. Whatever were the reasons for flying both canopies, the Russians soon decided that they were not all that important and by the beginning of World War II the habit had died out.

The Japanese

The Japanese used a military parachute which was a derivative of the Irvin, and the first experiments in 1941 were conducted with a static-line version of the Type 89 (1929) air-crew 'chute. It was quickly found that this was unsatisfactory, as was the later Type 97 (1937) model, although the canopy of this model was much better. From these experiments the Type 1 (1941) military 'chute emerged and this was used in their first paratroop operations in 1942. It was still not good enough, and in 1943 it was replaced by the Type 3 (1943) model which remained in use until the end of the war.

The Type 3 was a well-made parachute of modern design. The canopy was unchanged from the Type 97, being a 28ft diameter, of 28 gores, and shaped so that it flew almost as a hemisphere. A vent of 30in diameter was in the centre, and elastic cords pulled it in to an unloaded diameter of 8in. The material was silk, though some models used a mixture of natural and artificial fibres. It is not clear now whether the panels changed in porosity from hem to vent, but the presence of the elastic in the vent gives rise to the belief that they did not. There is some support for this in the fact that the shaped canopy was adopted in order to reduce oscillation, and oscillation becomes very noticeable when the gores do not have panels of graduated porosity. Porosity, for those unfamiliar with the term, is the ability of a piece of cloth to allow air to flow through it. A properly designed canopy is more porous towards the centre than it is at the hem; if it is not, then the air trapped inside it during the descent will spill out under the hem and cause severe oscillation. Most of the early parachutes suffered from this drawback.

The harness was made of dark-green silk webbing, with chromium-plated hardware and buckles. Great attention was paid to adjustable buckles to get a good fit, and the surprise of the design is that it has four body straps leading to a quick-release box which was much like that in the British GQ design. There were D-rings on the seat strap for attaching equipment.

The main pack closed at a single point, and was quite bulky, which must have been awkward in the cramped aircraft used for jumping. The static line pulled out a short closure pin from the pack eyelets, thus releasing the canopy. It then pulled out the main canopy by means of a loop attached to the apex and tied to the static line with a light break-line. There were probably several fatalities from this method of deployment, as it has now been shown that a single pin can easily jam in the eyelets, particularly if the man somersaults on leaving the plane. The surprising feature of this well-made parachute was that it used the single-point suspension method, although the Japanese must have known how unhappy the Germans were with this idea. However, the rigging lines were led to a large D-ring just behind the jumper's neck, and the harness culminated at this point too.

A 24ft reserve was carried on the chest and in order to allow time to use it in an emergency, the normal jump height was 1,000ft. However, the naval parachute-training programme

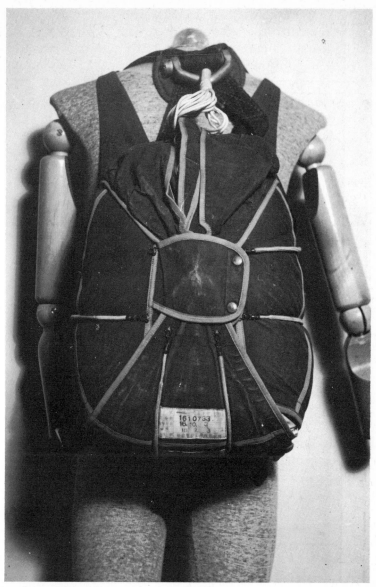

A wartime Japanese parachute, showing the way in which the rigging lines run to a single D-ring just behind the man's neck. (*Author*)

included two final jumps at 500 and 350ft, neither of which gave time to pull a reserve at all.

Trainee-parachutist towers were used in the early stages of training and the first jumps were from a height of 350ft with the rate of descent controlled by a line from the apex of the canopy. At the conclusion of the army training programme the men were dropped in high winds and on rough country – with what effect one can only surmise for such treatment rarely teaches much. The navy were more sensible, but insisted on the curious idea of the ultra-low jump.

Great Britain

The British started their airborne forces with less equipment than anyone. In 1936, prompted by the publicity given to the Soviet parachute troops, Raymond Quilter of the GQ Parachute Company offered a design for a practicable static-line parachute to the War Office. It would have been a good deal better than the German RZ, but the War Office could see no use for parachute troops and the offer was refused. Consequently, when Mr Winston Churchill demanded 5,000 parachute troops in 1940, there was little if anything to start from. For some years the RAF had given its aircrews 'parachute experience' by allowing them one or two jumps from the wing of a Vickers Valentia, or some similar machine. The pupils walked out on to the wing of the slow-flying plane, took hold of a strut, and pulled their ripcords. They were promptly whisked off into space, the more nervous ones still clutching their strut, or so it was always rumoured. In the warmth of a Middle East aerodrome like Habbaniyah or Almazar it wasn't too upsetting – provided one didn't make a habit of it. The War Office decided that a variation of this procedure would be a 'gentle way of introducing men to the act of parachuting' – as they naively put it in an instruction to the newly formed Central Landing Establishment.

Since there were only Whitley bombers at CLE, the pupils were taken up on a small platform projecting behind the tail where the rear gun turret had been originally. Here the instructor and pupil clung to a single railing while the pupil pulled his ripcord. It was terrifying and miserable experience, loathed by

A sequence showing the correct way to do a parachute landing roll. Note that the body absorbs the shock as the man curls round.

one and all. The parachutes used for this elementary exercise were ordinary Irvin aircrew back packs, and it took some time before Higher Authority could be persuaded to drop the pull-off method and experiment with a more useful means of exit. This was the floor hole of the Whitley, and for this the ripcord 'chute was useless. It was converted to a static-line operation by using a line to pull out the pins of the back pack. After 135 successful descents using this makeshift method, on 25 July 1940 a parachute failed completely to open, killing its wearer instantly. Immediately work was started on a safer parachute, and within five days a modification of Raymond Quilter's idea was translated into a working model. This was the first military parachute to have the rigging lines paying out before the canopy, and it used an Irvin canopy and harness with Quilter bags and packing. It worked, and the principle is used today on military parachutes all over the world. The sequence is shown in the diagrams of the 'Guardian Angel' for the principle is very similar. In essence what happens is that the static line breaks a number of thin restraining strings and pulls out the canopy in a closed bag from the back pack. This bag hangs above the parachutist as he falls away and in falling he draws out the rigging lines. On modern parachutes these lines are stowed in loops in separate pockets in the bag, but on some of the early models the idea of stowing the lines in the back pack was tried. This method was found to be more prone to twists and failures.

When the rigging lines have pulled out, the last 6in or so snaps a string tying the mouth of the canopy bag. The canopy can then pull out, periphery first, apex last. The apex is actually tied to the inside of the bag with another fine line, so in every jump there is one finite moment of time in which the parachutist is hanging below the aeroplane with the whole of his parachute in one long thin line above him, all drawn out by his weight. The final tie then snaps, and the canopy fills with air. This is the sequence of the X-type parachute, the one produced in five days in the late summer of 1940 by a small body of worried and harassed men at Ringway. At first it was called the 'Statichute', the X title coming later, but the changes over the years have been few, and most occurred in the first few months of its life. The one great virtue of the Statichute type of deployment is that it is virtually shock-free. The whole opening sequence is so smooth and progressional that the man feels no jerk at all, and the stories of parachutists landing with bruises on their shoulders and legs from the shock of opening has never applied to a man who jumped with a Statichute or its derivatives.

There were one or two accidents with the Statichute it is true, and once or twice it either failed to open or failed to disconnect. The tale is told of one guardsman who jumped from a Whitley and was 'hung up' on his 'chute, trailing miserably behind the tail and swinging and twisting in the slipstream. There was no way of hauling him in, nor any of getting him loose except by cutting his static line and sending him to certain death, so the pilot brought his Whitley in for the slowest possible landing that he could. Luckily this was not much more than 60mph with everything 'hanging out', and by slamming the brakes on as he touched down he was able to keep the landing run short. The crew leapt out and ran to the unfortunate parachutist who, so the story goes, staggered to his feet, gazed around him, gave a groggy salute and promptly fainted. Quite understandable in the circumstances – but probably apocryphal. Anyway he survived.

The most controversial aspect of the X-type parachute and its use by the British was the fact that until 1956 it was never backed up by a reserve 'chute. The Germans never used one

A British parachutist descending on his X-type parachute at night. The canopy panels and the harness are clearly visible. (*Imperial War Museum*)

either, for the same reason. The argument went that a reserve was undesirable because the main 'chute was perfectly safe. To carry a reserve meant that the man weighed more and so could carry less equipment. A reserve had to be carried on the chest, which was just where the British paratrooper carried his weapon container and personal equipment, and finally a reserve parachute meant that the dropping height had to be increased in order to give a man time to use it if he had to – and to increase the dropping height was not tactically sound. The Americans accepted all these limitations and carried reserves from the time they started airborne training, but the reserve never found favour in the British Army and as a result faith in the X-type was intense. Indeed so great was this faith that, even after the reserve was introduced, the troops who dropped on El Gamil airfield at Suez in 1956, discarded it and carried an extra belt of Vickers ammunition instead. With no reserve to worry about the dropping height was often very low, and for operations 500ft was quite normal and 350 has been quoted for some occasions. This latter figure sounds fairly risky, since it gives barely any time to release equipment, and no time at all if anything goes the least bit wrong with the opening of the parachute, such as twists in the lines.

The early wartime X-type parachutes were made from silk or rayon, both being materials which are sensitive to damp. This meant that some trouble had to be taken to dry them before storage and so elaborate air blowers were installed in parachute-packing sheds, and canopies had to be hung from frames in the roof for a specified time before storing. If they were packed damp, mildew and rot set in, and these were potentials for another and more sinister failing – damp-packed 'chutes often took longer to open than dry ones, the panels in the canopy tending to cling together, and the unfortunate parachutist might fall a long way before hearing the comforting sound of the silk opening above him. Later on, by 1944 and 1945, nylon became universal for canopies and these troubles disappeared. Nylon withstands an extraordinary amount of abuse, and does not suffer from the collection of static electricity to the same extent as does silk and rayon. Also, a nylon parachute can be packed while damp without ill effects pro-

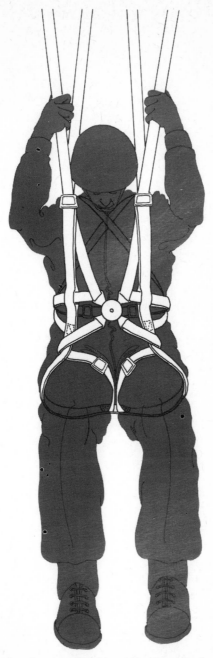

The X-type parachute harness. (David and Harrison VP Ltd)

vided that it is jumped soon afterwards. Nylon parachutes which land in trees are very rarely damaged, except by gross incompetence in their removal. Normally it is enough to pull the outer hem until the whole canopy comes to the ground, often bringing small branches with it. One would expect such treatment to put enough holes in the nylon to make it look like a colander, but it almost never happens that way. The author has seen a man actually swing on a canopy that was stuck in a pine tree, until his weight dragged it down, and it suffered no damage at all. Whatever benefits nylon may have brought in other fields, to the parachutist it has been a Godsend.

One other feature of the X-type deserves mentioning: the harness. The type and fit of his harness can be a matter of peculiarly personal importance to a parachutist, more so just at the moment when the canopy opens and everything tightens up. The X-type brought into being a harness which has survived to the present day without noticeable modification, and has now been copied in many other countries. It was evolved from the original Irvin harness on which the whole parachute was based. The X-type harness has four lift webs or risers, each running to a set of rigging lines. The lift webs are made in pairs and joined together with a U of webbing in which the parachutist sits. He is therefore in a sort of swing and, rather than a rope running up each side of his body, there are two lift webs; in place of a wooden seat, there are the same two lift webs running underneath his behind. The remainder of the harness is designed to make sure that he does not fall off the seat of the swing. To do this two straps are sewn to the 'seat' and pass between his legs, over the thighs, around the 'ropes' of the 'swing', and back to the front of the body at stomach level where they slot into a locking box. At chest level there is another webbing strap which acts in the same way as a belt and which also locks into the box. This 'belt' passes through loops in the ropes of the swing and prevents the parachutist from tipping off his seat, either forwards or backwards. That is all there is to it, although the finished article is a little more complicated than this simple description because the straps have to be ad-

The British exit, as used in the Whitley. A training jump through the hole in the floor of a balloon cage. (*Imperial War Museum*)

justable for different sizes of man, and there are modifications for attaching the parachute pack and the reserve. In fact the parachutist never actually sits in the seat of the swing because to do so would mean that his legs were sticking out in front and he would land in a sitting position. What he does is to push the seat behind him until he can stand straight up, but the support and the comfort is still there.

A peculiarity of the British is that trainees make their first jumps from a balloon. Balloons were introduced in 1941 in the days when aircraft were scarce. Someone remembered the observers of World War I who used their Guardian Angels when their balloons were shot down, and the idea was revived. The standard barrage balloon normally used to protect cities and other important targets from German bombers could be fairly easily made into a satisfactory captive load-carrying balloon, and the first tests were conducted with dummies at Cardington and Henlow. A very important feature of the argument in favour of the balloon was the fact that in the time required for one aircraft sortie one balloon could drop as many parachutists as could three Whitleys, and the absence of the slipstream and the difficult exit from the Whitley made it far easier for the student. The Central Landing Establishment was strongly in favour of the balloon, and pressed the Air Ministry for immediate manufacture. In fact wartime shortages held up the issues until early 1941, but from then on it has been used continuously. An official statement which recommended the introduction of the balloon cheerfully observed that 'the delayed opening produces an additional thrill.' This was no overstatement. Balloon jumping is an acquired taste, and some are never reconciled to it. It is a cold-blooded experience, devoid of the noise and distractions of aircraft jumping, and often long drawn out and unnerving. The balloon cage is no more than a plywood box with a canvas roof similar to an elementary covered wagon. It hangs below the gas bag on wires, with the main cable running in front of it to a bridle attached to the balloon.

The first cages were replicas of the Whitley exit, which meant that the floor was mostly a circular hole. The parachutists filed in and shuffled around the sides to sit in the corners and hang on like grim death to railings as they swayed up above the earth. Modern cages have a door exit which means that the students can stand on a much more solid floor, and a bar is locked across the door just in case anyone should be so foolish as to try and lean out of it. The cage holds four or five students and an instructor, and each man is hooked up as he enters. The cage then starts upward, leaving the ground with the most alarming lurches and swings. The door faces the tail of the balloon which is downwind, and this always means that the floor slopes down in that direction once again inducing the powerful tendency to hang on. The wind whistles through the canvas cover and in winter it is bitterly cold and the student is frozen within a few minutes. There is no other noise apart from the wind and the receding rumble of the winch truck. Conversation tends to lag on the way up, and dies away altogether at the top. The balloon stops with a slight jerk and promptly begins to sway about as the line tightens because it is now acting as a form of kite and the floor assumes an even more terrifying tilt. With no forward movement and no slipstream the parachutist drops straight down. The sense of urgency, of effort, and of companionship which exist in aircraft jumps are absent. Balloon jumps are strangely personal experiences and the long drop from the door is something one never forgets. Without the slipstream to assist in pulling out the parachute, one can feel every little tug as the ties break and the canopy comes out. Indeed, by looking up as one leaves the door, the whole sequence can be followed, from the glimpse of the instructor's face as one clears the door sill to the final rush as the sky fills with welcome nylon. The noise of that opening is quite distinct for some hundreds of yards, and at night it carries a cheerful message to those on the ground waiting for their turn.

A great advantage of the balloon is that it can be put up and used in a far smaller space than is needed for an aircraft drop zone. The Territorial Army use it in public parks and playing fields, and the preparation time is minimal. As a means of instructing student jumpers it is excellent because it gives a live jump onto a predictable landing spot. Using a loudhailer the instructor can call instructions to the student while he is in the air, and can follow his every action from leaving the door to ar-

riving on the ground. Another point in its favour is that it can often be used when aircraft are grounded for some reason or other, but the greatest reason for its continued use is that it is far less costly in time and money, and on that rests its reputation.

The great enemy of the balloon is lightning. The gas bag is filled with hydrogen, and a flash of lightning will ignite it almost explosively. This happened in 1961 culminating in the only award for gallantry to be earned in a parachuting balloon. The official citation reads as follows:

On the 14th May 1961, at Hornchurch, Sergeant Small was instructing parachutists in jumping from a cage supported by a balloon. The balloon exploded and the cage containing Sergeant Small and three men started to fall. Retaining his presence of mind he succeeded in dispatching two of them although the cage was tilted to nearly 45°. Even at this stage, as an experienced parachutist he could himself have jumped to safety but he remained to help the third man. The cage was now almost up-side down and falling rapidly but Sergeant Small gave clear and calm instructions to his pupil.

On impact both occupants of the cage suffered only minor injuries. This was a remarkable escape, particularly for the inexperienced parachutist who owed his life to the courage and devotion of his instructor.

Sergeant Small (now Captain Small), tells it somewhat differently, but the key point in his account is that he made his pupil climb up with him on to the framework of the top side so that they should not break their legs on hitting the ground. Neither did, the total injuries being a broken rib and ankle. Sergeant Small was awarded the George Medal.

The USA

The American Army started as late as the British in the airborne field. A Major William Lee was ordered to develop a programme for training and organizing airborne units in mid

British territorial parachutists waiting their turn for a balloon training jump. (*Keystone*)

1940. After a few weeks' intensive research he recommended the formation of a test unit to try out the available ideas and the result was the first airborne unit in the US Army, the Test Platoon. So well had Major Lee done his job, and so enthusiastic and knowledgeable was he about parachuting and airborne forces, that in due course, and fairly short course at that, he became a major-general and a man much revered in the memory of the US Airborne. The Test Platoon was forty-eight strong, formed of volunteers, all drawn from the 29th Infantry Regiment at Fort Benning. The platoon commander was Lieutenant William T. Ryder, with Lieutenant James T. Bassett as assistant. Their orders were both broad and challenging. In effect they were told to study the parachute and discover how best it could be used as a combat weapon.

From the very beginning they had troubles over equipment, and it was not for more than a year that these began to be eased, much less solved. There was no training equipment of any kind at Benning, so the platoon moved to New Jersey where there were two 250ft jump towers. These had been copied from the 'parachute tower' that had been put up at the 1939 New York World's Fair, where it had been a great success. These towers were fairly gentle affairs. For one thing they were too low to give a man more than a very brief flight, and the canopies were controlled by vertical wires around the rim, so that they could fall only straight downwards, and there was no chance to give the man a drift with the wind. In fact much effort had gone into making sure that the man did *not* drift, since these were for civilian use and safety was the overall consideration. The harness was unrealistic also, as it consisted of a basket-work seat, but a proper harness was soon fitted in and after two or three weeks the restraining wires were taken away and real free descents made. Having done this, the platoon was ready to try a descent from an aeroplane and returned to Benning. One of the towers followed them in due course, and was re-erected at Benning, where it remained until a few years ago, when a hurricane so severely damaged it that it had to be pulled down.

The first jump from an aeroplane took place on 16 August 1940 from a Douglas B-18 bomber over Lawson Field, Fort

Benning. The whole platoon made a demonstration mass jump on the 29 August, which was remarkable progress in only thirteen days. The demonstration was a complete success and convinced the high-ranking audience that there was a future for parachute troops.

The Test Platoon now fitted themselves with a modified Army Air Corps parachute, the T-4, which was rigged for static lines. This was an Irvin design with the then current three-hook fastening to the harness, and a large square back pack containing the canopy and lines. The canopy was 28ft diameter, flat circular, of conventional design and performance. The reserve, which was worn from the beginning, was a large chest pack hooked to the front of the harness with snap hooks. The rigging lines came out of the top of the pack and ran to the shoulders of the main harness where they joined to it. The handle was on the right. In existing photographs it seems as if the reserve was rather loosely attached, and it must have flopped about as all jumpers are seen holding it in to their stomachs, and there appears to be plenty of spare slack in the attachment straps. The T-4 worked well enough, even though it was a canopy-first-opening parachute, as were all aircrew life-saving 'chutes at that time.

Late in 1940 the first battalion was authorised – the 501st, and early in 1941 the Provisional Parachute Group was established under the direction of the former Major Lee, who was now a Lt Colonel. The Parachute Group produced training schedules, tactics, and recommended the equipment to be used. It also acted as a small experimental unit for new ideas. It was the driving force behind the formation of the Parachute School at Fort Benning, and the courses which it ran. Throughout these early months there were endless frustrations and delays. It took what the parachutists considered an unreasonable time to produce sufficient parachutes for them; for a long time recruiting to the new force was ahead of the manufacture of 'chutes. Aircraft were also short until some DC-3s

(*over page*) The American method of exit, jumping from a C-47 at Fort Benning, 1941. The short static line has quickly pulled out the T-4 canopy which is rapidly deploying in the slipstream. Static lines from the previous five jumpers lie along the fuselage. (*US Army*)

were bought. These were used with most of their civilian equipment still in them, even down to the seats in a few cases. A strong point cable was run down the ceiling of the cabin, the door removed and the hinges taped over. Later C-47s were hardly more sophisticated, but at least they had properly strengthened attachment points.

Training was severe because the American Army wanted its parachutists to be tough and to think tough. Tower jumps simulated the canopy opening by dropping the man for the length of a set of rigging lines before bringing him up short with a bone-jarring jerk – a process little better than the strappado of the Inquisition, and like the strappado it became more painful when repeated daily. This particular aspect of training was necessary to weed out the weaker brethren, and it continued to be used until the T-10 'chute was introduced in the late 1950s. A more sophisticated form of it was the 34ft tower. This had a door similar to that of a DC-3, and a horizontal wire running past it and above it. The trainee was attached to the wire by his harness, with several feet of slack line tucked into his pack. He then jumped out, fell until checked, and slid away along the wire until he hit the ground some yards away. It was a horribly painful experience, and not one that really gave the unfortunate student much idea of what jumping was like because it was far too coldblooded and painful. An actual jump never feels like the misery of training; there is always too much to be thinking about.

In 1941 the T-4 parachute was replaced by the T-7. This was an improvement in several directions. The T-7 was designed from the start to be a static-line parachute, and operated more reliably than the T-4. It was more comfortable to use, although nothing like the British X-type which was contemporary with it. It had a three-point harness, using snap hooks, and a wide canvas waistband to hold the pack close to the back. However, it was still canopy-first opening, and the shock was still there. The opening sequence was a little unusual as the canopy was retained in the pack by a sort of canvas 'lid', which was held to the outer cover by a breakable line running around the flaps. This shows more or less clearly in some of the photographs. This lid was firmly sewn to the static line and the apex of the canopy tied to it with a breakable line. The static line was stowed outside the pack, rather as the German RZ was, and, on extending, pulled the canopy clear of the pack by breaking the retaining line around the pack. After that the canopy developed much as every other similar parachute does, and it was quite quick in so doing. Photographs show the canopy streaming out very soon after the jumper has left the aeroplane, and in the jump into Noemfoor Island off the coast of New Guinea on 3 July 1944 something of a minimum height record was set up. Some of the drop planes were confused by a smoke screen, and misjudging the height, dropped their parachutists at 175ft above the ground. The trees on either side of the drop zone were at least 150ft high, and the men who fell into those were casualties. The others, who had a clear jump to the ground, were largely unhurt, although the overall casualties were 10 per cent of the total drop. These figures are astonishing, and they would probably never have been achieved with the British X-type, for that canopy would be barely starting to open properly after 175ft. The snap opening of the T-7 saved the unfortunate sticks who were so peremptorily launched into battle, and they must have agreed that the opening shock was worth it occasionally.

On a windy drop zone the T-7 was more difficult to get out of than the X-type. Neither had the shoulder releases of the later T-10, but the locking box on the X-type let go all the harness straps with one blow on the front. The T-7 required three separate snap hooks to be undone before the jumper was free, and this is not easy to do when being dragged at speed along rough ground. In Sicily in 1943 the 82nd AB Division suffered many casualties on the drop zones when it had to jump in winds of up to 35mph. In Greece in 1944 the 4th Battalion, the Parachute Regiment, jumped in winds described as 'gale force', and sustained 30–50 per cent casualties, many serious. In both cases injuries occurred as a result of men being dragged, though the reason for this may have been that they were hurt on landing, unable to wriggle out of their harness and would have to rely on someone else releasing them anyway. However, post-war T-7s were modified to take a single release box.

2 Containers, Kitbags and Platforms

Dropping the man by parachute is only half the story; if he is to be a useful soldier on the ground he must also take his weapons and equipment with him.

CONTAINERS

As the reader will now be painfully aware, in the beginnings of airborne thinking the problems of delivering men to the battlefield at all were sufficiently difficult to drive into the background the greater ones of delivering heavy equipment; leaving these to be solved at another time. For the most part the units had to devise their own methods, at least in British forces they did, and considerable ingenuity was shown by those who had only their native wit and experience to guide them. In other armies the pattern was similar.

Russia

The Soviets had a small range of practical containers in 1936 which took infantry small arms and ammunition; they probably also took mortars but there is no hard-and-fast evidence of this. The Soviets also tried very large containers since there is a film clip of 1935 or 1936 in existence showing a huge cylindrical container slung beneath the fuselage and in between the undercarriage legs of a ANT-6. The plane flies over the camera very slowly and very low, and at the moment of dropping a parachute canopy deploys from the rear of the container, perhaps operated by a manual release pulled from inside the fuselage, and as the canopy inflates the container is dropped away. It swings below its parachute and the plane flies on. How heavy was the container, what speed it fell at, what sort of shock-absorbing material was used are all unknowns, but it is a striking demonstration of forward thinking at a time when most nations were hardly considering the matter at all.

Another Soviet delivery method was to land a large plane carrying an external load, again slung between the legs of a fixed undercarriage. This was tried with vehicles and showed some success, so that in the Soviet occupation of the province of Bessarabia in 1941 a few small tracked vehicles were delivered in this way. Some propaganda use was made out of this operation and it was said that tanks had been brought in by air. This is highly unlikely, but nevertheless it was an imaginative and bold move. No more was heard of that method after 1941, and it may have been that it was all linked to the big ANT-6 monoplane which was already obsolete by that date. And, of course, vehicles were getting heavier and more difficult for low-powered aircraft to carry. Another pre-war Soviet experiment was intended to drop men without using parachutes. In the same film there is a short sequence in which another of the ANT-6 monoplanes flies slowly across the landing zone at an extremely low height, only 8–10ft off the ground, and slung between the undercarriage legs is a rectangular box. This has wheels on it, which resemble those on a motor cycle. The box, or, more appropriately, the carriage, is dropped and the plane flies off. The carriage runs along the ground losing speed rapidly, and when it stops it can be seen to be a series of metal cylinders arranged in a stack on the frame of the carriage so that they are at right angles to the direction of the plane's flight. The cylinders are about 2ft in diameter, and there are nine or ten on the vehicle. As the vehicle bumps to a stop two or three of the lids on the cylinders pop off, pushed from the inside, and out crawl smiling Soviet soldiers. One wonders if they were volunteers.

This intriguing military-circus act was never heard of again, and there is no mention of it in contemporary literature, but it was obviously not forgotten in Russia because it reappeared during the war in a slightly cruder and even more dramatic form. In the winter of 1942 there were many Russian partisan bands operating in the rear of the German army. They were particularly troublesome behind the German forces in the Orel salient, and they frequently cut communication links, attacked supply convoys, and raided small static units – classic partisan warfare in fact. The Germans retaliated and a running fight went on throughout the winter. It soon became apparent that the partisans were receiving reinforcements and supplies by air

An artist's impression of the pre-war Russian man-carrying free-fall trolley. Each cylinder contained one man.

from their own troops, and very occasionally the Germans captured a resupply drop zone. When they did, it was usual to try and decoy a resupply drop and capture it. This was only rarely successful, but on the occasion about to be related it was to yield far more than anyone could ever have foreseen.

A successful German raid had captured a drop zone in the middle of a clearing in the forest. There was deep snow and it was night; the temperature was well below freezing and the visibility good. When the drop came in it was carried in the old ANT-6 monoplanes, which were by that time so hopelessly outclassed that they could only survive by flying at night in the more remote parts of the front. They flew in very low and very slow and each one dropped a succession of boxes and bundles, some through the doors, some from under the wings. The boxes, it was noticed, were all carried as under-wing stores; the bundles came through the doors. The ANT-6s were allowed to lumber off home and the Germans came out to see what they had gained. To their astonishment it was not a resupply drop, it was a reinforcement exercise. Each box and each bundle contained a man, who was lying helplessly in his container waiting to be released.

It had been done in the following way. Each box was crudely made from local timber and filled with straw. One man crawled into the middle of the straw and the lid was clipped on. The straw provided not only a shock-absorbing medium, but it also prevented him from freezing to death on the short flight to the drop zone. The bundles were large sacks also packed with straw and with their mouths loosely tied up; presumably the sack men were luckier than the box men as one assumes that they would have been able to have their heads out during the flight, and would only have 'battened down' at the last moment. But this is conjecture; the Germans could waste no time in interrogating their prisoners and none survived. The incident was recorded and there is no mention of it in any other combat report, so that it is safe to assume that it was an uncommon method of despatching men to the rear-area war.

After this ingenious and effective start the Soviets appear to have virtually abandoned any effort to produce a standard method of dropping equipment to their airborne forces, and for the most part their parachute troops were sent into action with little more than small arms and grenades. Certainly the few parachute operations which were mounted by the Soviet Army in World War II were all of them badly planned, badly led, badly conducted, and the troops were badly equipped. The Germans had little difficulty in rounding them up on each occasion. There is some evidence to show that small numbers of weapons containers were made and used, but these were only small and light in construction, and carried only the basic infantry-support weapons and some ammunitition. The ability to drop heavier equipment was apparently completely ignored. The scene changed markedly after World War II when there was much interest in airborne warfare, although until the late 1950s there was little apparent movement towards effective delivery of heavy weapons.

The main reason for the Soviet delay in producing proper heavy drop gear lay in their aircraft. The Li-2 (derived from the DC-3) was suitable only for dropping under-wing or door loads and this plane was the only practical transport aircraft available until the middle 1950s. After that there was a number of machines which could drop heavy loads through tail-opening doors and, having built these, the Soviets set about evaluating the Western methods of dropping large items of military equipment.

The mention of the Soviet attempts to drop men without parachutes prompts a small diversion from the main stream of this chapter to deal with this rather specialised subject for a short while, for there is more to it than may be thought. In the early years of the war the successes of the German parachutists directed all thinking into using this method of getting troops to battle, but when the glider came into use it was seen what an expensive and wasteful tool a parachute is. The training needed is really alarming and the specialisation of equipment inordinately complicated. A glider could carry any soldier and the only training he needed was in how to get in and out, a simple enough drill for everyone. The drawback to the glider was the fact that it was an aircraft and needed piloting, furthermore it was slow and cumbersome and took up a great deal of space on an aerodrome. It, too, was expensive.

But if equipment could be dropped in boxes, mused some genius, then why not men? It all seemed simple. What was needed was a wooden box containing seats for six or eight men, some shock-absorbing device on the underside and several parachutes to lower it. The box could be carried slung underneath the parent plane, dropped onto a small drop zone with great precision, and there would be a complete tactical subunit with all its weapons and ammunition, ready for action. Put like that it looked attractive and there was more than one drawing-board design during the war years. Luckily for the troops it never came to anything, but it was renewed again in the late 1940s and the GQ Parachute Company even went so far as to build a mock-up of their ideas on the subject. They suggested a neat streamlined egg-shaped car carrying six men, to be carried in the bomb bay of large bombers. To a man the Parachute Regiment declared that they would never go near the thing and it quietly died away. There were a number of similar schemes, one or two intending to use rotors or retro rockets instead of parachutes, but they all faded out without even experimental models being built.

And now back to the history of containers.

Great Britain

In the British Army there was virtually no pre-war experience to draw upon, except for some very limited RAF supply dropping dating back to the small-scale tribal revolts in Northern

India and Iraq. In 1939 the RAF had two simple equipments for dropping stores. One was a small metal container about 30in long and 12in diameter, with a lid at one end. It could carry up to 150lb and had a 10ft parachute attached to the other end. The second was a wooden beam to which small boxes or crates were tied. The beam had a 14ft parachute on it, but its load was little more than 150lb. Both these elementary devices were meant to be carried in the bomb bays and could not be dropped at speeds greater than 120mph. The speed restriction was hardly decisive, but the size and shape of both containers made them of little use to the fledgling airborne units. Neither would accept a rifle or machine-gun, and both took time to unpack on the ground. The Central Landing Establishment was, therefore, tasked with the requirement for a new series of containers.

The first one was only a marginal improvement. It was a thick canvas mat, quilted to give some measure of shock absorption and stiffened with wooden poles. Pockets were sewn into the inside to accept equipment, and these were long enough to take rifles and machine-guns. To pack the container the mat was simply rolled up and strapped to a bar which carried the parachute. This was an ordinary 28ft diameter X-type which fitted into a pack at one end of the bundle. Once again the container was dropped from a bomb bay or a bomb cell, and this was a restriction on what the CLE could produce. The rolled mat was not considered a success, despite the fact that it could carry about 200lb, and it was abandoned. The US Army, on the other hand, used a very similar bundle until the late 1940s with no apparent difficulties.

The next design looked to be better; it was a box made for a bomb cell, but it was bigger and more robust. An initial batch were 6ft long and 15in diameter, of wood and metal, and circular in section. Unfortunately, the GQ Parachute Company, who made them, left no opening apart from the ends, and the first one had to be packed by lowering a small boy into it head first. For all that it worked, and the next models had a side opening; finally they were hinged all along their length and were opened and packed and unpacked in two halves. This became the well-known CLE (from the initial letters of the Cen-

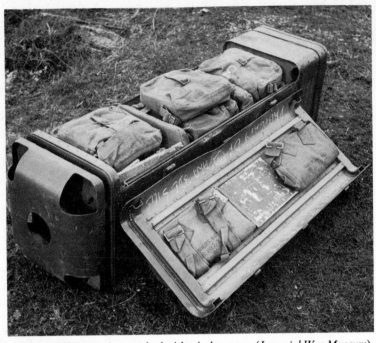

A British CLE container packed with wireless gear. (*Imperial War Museum*)

tral Landing Establishment, which designed it) container, which was used on most of the early airborne operations of the British Army, particularly for resupply and the delivery of stores to clandestine groups such as the Maquis in France. The CLE would carry up to 600lb, and landed without damaging its contents on one end which had a crushable metal pan to absorb the shock. Later on in the war it was decided that if containers were to be dropped from bombers it would be as well if they were the biggest that the plane could take, and so some monsters as long as 11ft were made for four-engined machines. Even so these did not carry everything, and radio sets were a constant headache to the container designers. No sooner was a container adapted to a particular set than the set was modified and the dimensions were changed.

It is hardly surprising that the CLE looked for some variable container to take all loads, and set about producing what ultimately became one of the better known items of resupply equipment, the wicker pannier. This would carry almost any man-portable weapon in the infantry armoury, or an infinite variety of other equipment. It could not be hung on a bomb rack, and had to be pushed through a door, but it worked splendidly, and some are still in service. The pannier was adaptable to many other more mundane uses, and the pilferage rate was always high. For dropping, a 10 or 16ft parachute was strapped on to the top, a static line hitched to the aircraft, and the pannier was simply pushed out when the time came. It was simple and cheap. But the road to it had been fairly long, and even the pannier could not cope with a vehicle and guns.

Many surprisingly awkward loads were carried in bomb bays. Motor-cycles were surrounded with a wooden crate which took most of the stresses of flight and landing, yet were easily removed on the drop zone. The motor-cycle had to lie on its side in the bomb bay, but turned upright as the parachutes opened and this gave some trouble. Folded airborne pedal cycles were easier as they just had a parachute strapped to them and then they were thrown out of the door. It was quickly found that the obvious way of landing them, that is to say on their wheels, was very wrong indeed as it never failed to produce a banana-shaped wheel, and the handlebars were finally selected as being best able to take the shock. Even carrier pigeons were dropped, in their case in small baskets carrying four birds in individual partitions, though whether they were ever used operationally seems unlikely.

The USA

In the US Army containers were used from the very beginning of the formation of airborne forces. As has been mentioned, the first models were a rolled bundle, and that type, together with variations on the basic theme, continued for many years. At the same time numerous experiments were tried in the search for the best design, and containers in all shapes and sizes appeared in the years between 1940 and 1943, finally settling into a small family which looked not too far different from all the others then in use. Because of the US reluctance to use kitbag containers on the man, these containers remained in

A captured German weapons container with wheels and towing handle fitted. The circular ring on the near end is the stowage for the canopy. Inside are supports for two rifles and an assortment of equipment, probably signalling gear. (*US Army*)

Three German parachutists, about 1941. The RZ harness and static line are clearly shown. Note the cut-down helmet, knee pads and lace-up boots. The man on the left is wearing the late-pattern camouflaged overall, the other two are not. (*Bundesarchiv*)

service until about 1950, when they were beginning to prove more than obsolete.

Germany

The Germans really pioneered the use of containers, and throughout the war continued to use them for personal weapons. Their arms containers (known as *Waffenhälter*) were similar to the British ones, so much so that one is led to suspect that the British copied them for their own design. They were long metal canisters which were carried in special racks in the bomb bay of the Ju-52 and in some cases they were slung under the wings. The design had not been finalised by the time of the Crete operation and there were then three or four different sizes which were graded according to the load they had to carry. Soon after Crete the design was standardised on one model. This was 5ft long, square in section, and 16in across the width. There was a full-length lid held on by clips and four straps which buckled all round the container. At the top end a parachute was attached and folded into a small canvas pack which was the same diameter as the container. Some of these canopies were specially made cargo 'chutes, but some were elderly man-carrying versions. These latter gave a lower rate of descent, but lasted only a few drops.

Loaded, the container weighed a maximum of 260lb. A single platoon required fourteen of these containers to carry all its weapons and ammunition into battle, although it must be remembered that the platoon strength in a German parachute battalion was forty-three men when up to strength. With that number of men looking for their containers it was most necessary to clearly mark each one and this was done with coloured stripes around one end – usually, but not invariably, the top end. The lower end had a corrugated metal shock absorber attached to it, and this could be replaced for subsequent landings if the container was recovered. Indeed the difficulties of making sufficient containers in wartime was such that the Luftwaffe had a special recovery and salvage unit whose sole job was the collection and refurbishing of airborne equipment abandoned on the drop zone. Their main task was naturally in training exercises, but they were also shipped into the war zone

Two Germans haul a container off the dropping zone.

as soon after the operational assault as possible. In Crete this unit came fairly late after the fighting because of the difficulties of travelling right across the Balkans with their transport and the lack of shipping to Crete. By the time they reached Crete much of the attractive and useful gear had been either ruined or stolen so that the recovery rate was low. It was one more expense in an already costly battle.

The containers were padded with assorted pieces of felt and sorbo rubber to fit whatever load was in them. One item which was common to all was a pair of wheels with which to roll the loaded box off the drop zone should this be necessary; there were also two folding carrying handles on each side.

This design of container remained in service throughout the war, though it was used less and less frequently as the prospect of actual airborne warfare diminished for the *Fallschirmjaeger*. In the final drop in the Ardennes offensive there are conflicting reports of containers being used, but Colonel von der Heydte did take a signal platoon with radios, and the only way that the radio sets could have come in was in containers. On that occasion the containers failed utterly and all the sets were smashed, but that was not entirely the fault of the equipment: the winds were too high and the ground far too rugged for any successful parachute landing.

The failings of the containers, in particular the time taken to unload them, led to some attempts to carry weapons on the man. These never progressed very far, for two reasons. One was the prevailing lack of interest in purely parachute operations after Crete, the other was the unsuitability of the German parachute and its harness. A man landed so roughly that it was essential that he was unencumbered and free to twist and roll. Crete had shown that time spent on the actual drop zone was not only wasted, it was often fatal and the several minutes needed to unpack containers could be most damaging to a unit. All that the defender had to do was to lay an aim on a container and pick off the parachutists as they ran up to it. With no more than a pistol or a sub machine-gun with which to fire back – and a limited supply of ammunition – the parachutists were more or less helpless. Had the Germans pursued the airborne army further into the war there would undoubtedly have been some major improvements to their personal equipment and the carriage of weapons into battle, but it never happened.

The Home Guard anti-invasion manuals which appeared in England in 1940 stressed the importance to the defenders of getting to grips with the parachutists before they had time to locate their containers, collect their weapons, rally, and become an effective fighting force. On at least one occasion the German paratroopers overcame this hazard by landing right on top of their objective and rushing directly to it firing their pistols as they went. Surprise won the day, but it could not be relied upon to do it every time, and they never overcame the handicap of the container.

KITBAGS AND VALISES

The British and Americans quickly realised the tactical drawback to a system which forced the soldier to find and unpack a container before he was properly armed and equipped. It could easily happen that the container became hooked up in the aircraft and was carried all the way back to base again, or it might collide with the man during his descent (no small hazard from the Whitley), or it might be dropped by some mishap miles from the man's drop zone and fall into the hands of the enemy. Even in the best circumstances he might spend as long as half an hour looking for it, and at night the job was virtually impossible.

The first difficulty to overcome was the overloading of the man and danger of injury on landing. Quite early on in the formation of the British airborne it was found that a man could parachute with a load almost equal to his own weight without difficulty, provided that it was suspended beneath him in flight and hit the ground in time to allow his parachute to resume a normal shape before he himself arrived. The result of this discovery was the kitbag and the weapon valise. The weapon valise was an envelope of thick felt material, roughly sewn along the seams and fitted with straps. There were two sizes, one for rifles and one for light machine-guns, each very similar in outline. The weapon was placed inside the valise and the pocket strapped up. A 20ft rope was attached from the para-

chute harness to the mid point of the valise, so that it hung horizontally, and the weapon would hit the ground all along its length rather than at one end. In the latter case there was a distinct liability that the butt or fore end could be badly damaged. The valise was held to the man by two body straps, one round the neck, and one round the right leg. The right hand came across and gripped the left side of the valise, the left hand the right. The free end of the attachment rope was looped on to the right-hand leg strap of the parachute harness, and a small canvas sleeve slid along it. This sleeve was most important, and there was a loop on it through which the right hand went when gripping the container. Its use will become apparent later. The neck and leg straps were pulled tight by sliding buckles and secured by quick-release pins, both of which were on the same piece of line.

The best way to describe the use of all these items is to follow a jumper through the door. As the stick moves down the plane he moves with it, swinging his right leg with its awkward load and shuffling the left to keep ahead of it, much as a boxer or fencer keeps his leading foot forward. Arriving at the door the jumper gripped his valise a bit tighter and jumped into the slipstream holding hard to prevent it being torn away from him. Luckily the C-47 was kind in this respect, and only later with faster and more powerful planes was the risk increased to a real hazard. As soon as his 'chute was open and his anti-collision drill over, the parachutist started to lower his valise. A quick tug on the line joining the quick-release pins cleared them from their strap lockings, and jumpers were taught to run their hand to the end of the line and actually look at the pins and see that they were really free. There was good reason for this. An anxious man could easily not pull one or the other out. If he left the lower one in and started to lower the valise it turned upside down and locked against his leg by the lower strap. It was then impossible to release and the man had no option but to land with it in this awkward position; quite often it meant a broken leg – so that lower pin had some significance.

An American officer emplaning for D-day, carrying a staggering burden of equipment all of which will land with him. His load contrasts with the clean outline of German parachutists. (*US Army*)

However, both pins out, a quick look below, and he began to lower the valise. The canvas sleeve was gripped tightly in the right hand and pointed up to the sky. The left hand supported it. In this position the rope was pretty well jammed in the sleeve and did not move. By dipping the outer end downwards the rope would slide through, and the skill was now to play it slowly through the sleeve without letting it run away and take charge. In a way it was rather like playing a fish. To let the rope run was fatal, it ripped through the sleeve and in a second was going too fast to ever stop. In another second the sleeve became nearly red hot from the friction and there was nothing for it but to let go. Sometimes the rope broke. But this was rare with the valise which was never more than 30 or 40lb (kitbags proper often broke loose). On reaching the end of the line, the valise swung gently until landing, when it was immediately available to its owner, who merely pulled in the suspension line. He could, therefore, recover it even when lying down in the pitch dark, in fact without ever seeing it.

The kitbag was a heavier version of the valise. Fully packed, it was meant to be 2¼ft long and 1ft in diameter, but it frequently exceeded these sizes. It was made of strong canvas, reinforced with leather, with an opening at one end and a padded shock absorber at the other. It would take radios, batteries, ammunition, anything at all – even the padre's collapsible field altar and field communion set, together with his minimum vestments and an airborne water bottle of communion wine. The quoted maximum load was 80lb, but this was often exceeded, though not without risk. The pad at the bottom had a recess on the outside for the parachutist's foot to fit into, and when he stood up the whole weight of the kitbag rested on the floor and not on his foot. To walk down the plane he picked it up by swinging his body to the left side, and heaved his right leg forward, chanting the while 'kitbag – kitbag', so that the whole stick kept in step. The kitbag was attached to the right leg by the same type of quick-release strap as the valise. The upper one went round the thigh, the lower round the ankle, but the dangers of not releasing both pins together remained. On reaching the door the best way to get out was to simply throw the kitbag over the sill. The thrower followed willy-nilly. Once

The dreaded kitbag hazard.

A British sergeant ready to jump with his kitbag. His small pack hangs on his chest, under his outer smock and harness. His kitbag is strapped to his right leg and attached to him by a rope. Taken about 1944. (*Imperial War Museum*)

clear, and with his parachute open, he followed the same drill, only this time it was more than ever necessary to take care over the lowering – 80lb was far more likely to take charge if treated with contempt. A free-falling kitbag arrived on the drop zone with much the same effect as a small bomb and earned the dropper some very black marks indeed. On training jumps a court of inquiry was convened to write off the stores carried in the kitbag, and many a court has been astonished at the staggering amount of valuable and bulky items that was solemnly listed as being destroyed, and many a quartermaster has greeted the news of a kitbag disaster with joy and relief.

After the war the kitbag was developed to carry loads for which it had never been designed to do, and 3in mortars were loaded into it. The barrel of the weapon made up one load, and stood up so high out of the bag that it came level with a man's chin. He put his arm around it and clutched it close to him as the chute opened, finally lowering it with great care. But by that time the canvas sleeve had gone and in its place was a simple shock-absorber device hitched to the parachute harness, and this meant that once clear of the plane the kitbag could be kicked away off and left to lower itself. This was a substantial step forward.

The US Army developed a similar weapon carrier to the valise, known as the Griswold container. It was not lowered below the jumper, but carried down on the man all the way. The US parachute allowed a slow enough rate of descent for this to be safe, and on landing the parachutist rolled over it. On other occasions smaller weapons were carried in the harness straps behind the reserve, and in 1942 a smaller container was developed for weapons carried in this way. There was also some interchange of equipment between the Allied armies, for just as US airborne forces used Horsa gliders on occasions, so did they take on a few British kitbags. Certainly the 513th Parachute Battalion had some in 1945, and probably used them in the Rhine crossing operation.

Post-war research was directed towards a fool-proof kitbag which would carry everything, including weapons and equipment. It was some years before it was produced, but there have now been several models of what is substantially the same item. It is now a sort of parcel made of canvas which adapts itself to the load it has in it, rather than the other way about, and it is carried and secured to the man in a similar way to the US Griswold container. Now, however, the nightmare of lowering has gone, and in its place is a very strong nylon rope which stretches to take up the shock of the falling load. But the principle is still the same, and the man has still to lift and carry this heavy and sometimes bulky object to the door of the plane.

Of the nations who had airborne forces during World War II only the British and Americans developed these methods of carrying personal weapons and equipment. The story of the Soviets and Germans has been related, and the Japanese never seem to have got farther than folding rifles and sub machine-guns zipped into a canvas chest pack. Yet the efficient carriage of the soldier's equipment was really at the heart of the airborne secret, and it is strange to see how it was grasped by only one side.

Despite the apparent lead that the Soviets had in dropping all types of container before the war, they never pursued the subject, and it remained for the Allies to perfect the technique. The ultimate success did not come until long after the war was over, but by 1945 a certain amount of ground work had been completed. Jeeps and anti-tank guns were dropped from bombers using special 32ft canopies in clusters. The jeep was fitted with elaborate frames above and below the vehicle to take the strains of both the parachute opening and the landing. Various connectors helped the chassis to accept the unexpected shocks, and crash pans were rigged below to absorb the landing. The 6-pounder anti-tank gun was rigged in the same way, though as its construction was more robust a simpler framework could be used. Both jeep and gun were hung in the bomb bay of a bomber from which the bomb doors had been removed. They hung well out into the slipstream making plenty of drag with their square shapes, and because of this shape they did not always fall straight. There was a tendency to somersault, and many tricks were tried to overcome this. One evil effect of a somersault was the cutting of rigging lines, and sometimes the collapse of a canopy. On rare occasions the entire suspension system was cut away and the whole load 'can-

A crated jeep in the bomb bay of a Halifax. Crash pans and shock-absorbing structure are bolted under the jeep axles. About 1944. (*Imperial War Museum*)

dled' into the drop zone. All manner of methods were used in combating the somersault menace, the most obvious one being to round off all the corners on the load so that rigging lines did not catch, and the somersault became harmless. A better idea was to tilt the load slightly forward and use the slipstream to correct the first tendency to roll. Jeep trailers were especially prone to somersaulting, and the cure was not found until 1952, by which time the four-engined bombers had gone and the Handley Page Hastings had replaced them as the load carrier for airborne forces.

The crash pan and framework method of heavy dropping was a clumsy and difficult way of taking a small gun or vehicle to the dropping zone: the rigging of the load took a long time and demanded highly trained men, the aeroplane needed special equipment, the aerodynamics of the plane were dis-

Sections of a 75mm airborne gun in their parachute loads under the wing of a C-47. The gun's crew have taken the opportunity to add a few additional items to the bundles. About 1944. (*Imperial War Museum*)

turbed, the success of the drop could not be assured, and in the event of a hang up or cancellation of the drop the plane could not possibly land with the load still in place. Having said all that, the next methods to appear still suffered from many of the same drawbacks.

PLATFORMS

The most significant change in the capability of parachute troops since the war has been in the field of heavy-equipment dropping. As has already been told, gliders were an enormously expensive and wasteful means of getting vehicles, guns and ammunition to the battle. It was imperative that some

(*over page*) October 1950. The 187th Regimental Combat Team emplaning in a C-119 for their jump near Pyongyang, North Korea. Apart from the aircraft, there is virtually no change from the equipment of 1945. (*US Army*)

means be found of parachuting these heavy loads along with the men. The dropping beams and crated loads were no more than half an answer and it was not until the tail-loading air-craft of the 1950s came into military service that a proper solution was found. In its simplest form the solution was a wooden board with a load tied to it and a parachute or cluster of parachutes tied to the load. The board allowed the load to be pushed into the body of the aeroplane when it was being loaded on the ground, and it also acted as a skid when the load was being pushed out in the air. The method of dropping was to fly with the tail doors off, and when over the drop zone to point the nose into the air and allow gravity to pull the loaded board out. A static line deployed the parachutes. All the pull of the canopy was taken by the load itself, and some straw or cor-rugated cardboard absorbed some of the shock on landing.

Quite obviously such a crude arrangement needed con-siderable sophistication in actual use, but that is the basic prin-ciple of the 'skid-board' or 'suspended-load' technique and it has been widely used by many nations, particularly the US and France. It has the great advantage of simplicity and cheapness; there is very little to go wrong, and training is easy. But like everything else it has its drawbacks. Whilst the actual skid board is admittedly cheap it imposes considerable strains on its load both when the parachutes deploy and when the board lands. To deal with the former the load usually has to be strengthened at the attachment points, and if that load is a vehicle, then there is additional cost in doing that, cost that is hidden from that associated directly with dropping. The shock of landing is also considerable, the more so with a loaded vehicle carrying its battle gear, so the axles and springs have to be enlarged also. Even so, it is common for the vehicle casual-ties to be quite high in a skid-board drop, since the shock-absorbing medium cannot be too thick or too powerful or the vehicle would never get on to it nor off it. Indeed the author has watched the frantic efforts of a French crew struggling to get their jeep off a skid board after a hard landing when the compressed straw underneath had jammed under the chassis and was lifting the wheels just clear of the board.

For other items, such as food or ammunition, the skid board

can be immensely useful, and its great advantage lies in the fact that the board is so cheap that it is left on the drop zone with never a second thought. For this sort of load the contents are contained within straps which take the pull of the parachute or parachutes.

It is common practice to use more than one canopy for these heavy loads: a single canopy would have to be so huge to carry the weight that it would be quite unmanageable; also, single canopies oscillate but multiple canopies do not – they fly in a very stable manner. Finally, with multiple canopies, should one fail to open or only partly open, the load will not be entirely destroyed, but with one canopy the slightest failure could be the end of that platform.

It is now not usual to drop the load out of the plane by tilting up the nose. The modern practice is to pull it out either by deploying the main canopies and letting them stream out behind, or by deploying a special extractor chute which pulls out the load and then acts as a static line and pulls off the bags from the main chutes. These opening operations require rather more than a simple static line to work them satisfactorily, and all these platforms have quite complicated clockwork timing devices which release the various functions in the correct sequence as the load leaves the plane.

The British and the Soviets use a more complicated and expensive method for their heavy equipment. This is known as the 'stressed platform'. A stressed platform is a large skid board made of alloy girders. The parachutes are attached to the platform and the shock absorber is put below it. The load carries no strain at all beyond the reduced bump on landing. Ordinary unmodified vehicles can be successfully dropped on a stressed platform and quite delicate loads – even on one occasion eggs – can be put down on the ground without harm.

A stressed platform is expensive, complicated and fairly heavy. It takes away some of the available carrying capacity of the transport aeroplane, and it has to be recovered from the drop zone. It may often have to be refurbished after the drop

(*over page*) May 1962. A French heavy drop load landing during Exercise Colibri. The photographer has caught the load at the instant that the disconnect has released the canopies (*Keystone*)

and in any case it will need to have its shock-absorbing airbags renewed before it can be used again. The loading and rigging of a stressed platform is an esoteric art requiring careful training, and the loads are susceptible to slight damage if the precise methods are not followed; but this is not entirely confined to stressed platforms, for skid boards require careful packing also. However, the rigid platform is troublesome to load correctly and it has to be balanced precisely to hang squarely.

For the army prepared to face the trouble and expense of rigid platforms the advantages are encouraging. The most obvious one is that there is little restriction on what can be put on the platform – only size and weight determine the limits. There is no need to build special vehicles and guns; damage on the drop zone is less than with skid boards (given equal weather conditions); and derigging the loads and getting them into action is invariably faster by a large margin. A load of 32,000lb has been successfully dropped on a stressed platform and the British Army habitually drops Ferret scout cars on them.

The expense of the platform lies not only in its construction, but in its liability to damage. The alloy girders which make up the main frame are very carefully designed to give the greatest rigidity for their weight. The parachutes are attached by steel cables which are shackled to D-rings on the edges of the frame, and these cables are led up over the load to a central suspension point where there is a 'disconnector' whose purpse will become clear in a moment. The parachutes are attached to the upper side of the disconnector. Below the platform are plywood doors which are held shut by pins. These doors hold the air bags in place. There are attachment points all round the platform to which the load is held, and to which restraining ties are connected when the load is in the aeroplane's hold. Without these restrainers the whole platform would move about the floor in flight.

The sequence of dropping is quite complicated and enormously impressive to watch from inside the hold. All planes which drop platform loads are tail-loaders. The older models such as the Beverly and the C-119 flew with their doors off when dropping platforms, but later machines such as the C-

130 can open their door in flight, which adds enormously to their speed and the comfort of the crew inside. The first action is to release the extractor 'chute. This is usually about 10ft in diameter and it streams over the door sill and instantly develops an enormous pull. Within a second or two the load begins to move, accelerating violently and making a roaring noise like an express train as it goes. The side restraining ties fall away and it tips over the edge of the door. A clockwork delay actuated by the extractor 'chute releases the main canopies after the platform is clear of the plane and dropping freely, whereupon the extractor acts as a static line and pulls the main canopies out of their bags. They now stream out above the platform like enormous paper bags, slowing the headlong descent and swinging the platform into the horizontal. They do not open immediately, but fly with their mouths held partly closed by a special reefing gear. This is done to give all the canopies a chance to get clear of their bags and fully stream out; after two seconds the reefing gear releases them and all canopies open together.

The platform is now falling at a steady speed, hanging quite steadily under its cluster of white canopies, but complications are not over yet. After another time interval another clockwork device opens the plywood doors under the platform and the air bags drop down and fill with air. The air bags are made of a synthetic material and are stubby cylinders in shape. They fill with air at atmospheric pressure through a large hole in their lower surface. A platform has eight such bags, four to each side. On landing, the bags burst with a loud bang – it can be heard several miles away on a still night – and absorb practically all the shock. At the same time the disconnect on the parachute cables releases itself and the canopies can drift harmlessly away. If they remain attached there is a very real danger of the load being overturned by a gust of wind.

After all this it merely remains for the derigging crew to run up and release the holding-down ties on the load and pull it off. If the load is a vehicle it can be driven off the platform within a very few seconds of the crew reaching it – indeed the speed of some crews is quite remarkable, and half a minute would be thought to be a poor performance.

The Soviet version of this platform is almost identical with the British one except that most models, though not apparently the latest ones, have two rigid metal bars which swing above the load, and to these bars the parachutes are attached. Every other feature seems to be an exact copy of the British platform, and the air bags and disconnects certainly appear to work in the same way. There is however, one particular native feature on the Soviet model. When it is carrying an overload, one that is above the normally safe limit of the canopies used, a set of retro-rockets is fitted to the disconnect shackle above the load. Retro-rockets are perfectly normal solid-fuelled rockets which fire in the opposite direction to the one in which they are travelling, and so they act against their motion and slow it down. This is the secret of the Soviet platform. When the air bags open, a weighted line drops below the platform; this line is the trigger for the retro-rockets. When the weight strikes the ground the rockets fire and burn for about a second, exerting a considerable braking effect on the load. Just as they burn out, the air bags reach the ground and the landing is quite normal, even though the load may be up to 50 per cent greater than the normal top limit of the canopies.

Although retro-rockets have often been considered as an extra braking effort by other nations, or even as a complete replacement for the parachute, they have not previously been successfully used, and much credit must go to the Soviets for being the first to do it as a practical operation.

In recent years research has been directed towards dropping at lower altitudes to reduce the time of flight. Both the British and Americans have been trying an ultra-low-level delivery method in which the main parachutes are deployed as the plane flies across the drop zone at a height of about 50ft. The canopies stream out behind the tail and quickly develop, pulling the load clear quite quickly. Once clear the idea is to allow it to swing just enough to be upright as it touches the ground. In an extension of this idea the load is jerked out at a height of about 10ft and there is no vertical restraint at all – the load, on its skid board, actually drops straight to the ground and the parachutes serve to slow it only in a forward direction. Even so, loads dropped by this method tend to arrive at a brisk forward speed and slide along for some yards in a disconcerting manner. As always, piloting skill is called for to a high degree. Flying straight, level and low at a slow speed is never easy, and to have the additional hazard of a quick major change of weight and centre of gravity at the same time must be as much as most pilots wish to take on.

It would be foolish to try and pretend that it is easy to put a heavy load on to the ground using parachutes. It is a complicated and time-consuming operation demanding considerable skill in the rigging and setting up of the loads and their parachute equipment, the right type of aeroplane, and a large amount of specialised equipment both on the ground, in the mounting area and in the plane itself. The training of the men involved takes time, and the skills have to be maintained by continual practice. The entire system costs money and effort. From the very beginnings of heavy dropping there have been attempts to devise some other means of delivering the loads to the drop zone. All manner of folding wings and rotor blades have been put forward; but they all suffer from a fundamental failing of some sort, and that failing is usually far less attractive than the known ones suffered by parachutes. Wings are bulky and rely on mechanical locking to hold them. Rotor blades are the same, with the additional difficulty that they may be strained or broken by the opening shock.

The parachute still offers the most reliable, the cheapest, and the simplest method of delivering a large weight from the sky without landing the machine that is carrying it. It looks as though it will for many years yet.

3 Special Weapons

Special forces usually demand special weapons. This has been happening since the first of the ancient charioteers discovered that he had to cut down the shaft of his javelins if he was to throw them from his vehicle. The demand for short javelins was not too difficult to fulfil; nowadays anyone who asks for special weaponry is liable to find it much more of a struggle to get what he wants.

In the early days of airborne forces – that is the mid 1930s – there was a good deal of glamour and mystery attached to parachute troops. The Germans in particular boosted the image of their parachutists to that of supermen, and quite naturally the supermen demanded super weapons. The Russians, on the other hand, seem to have approached their airborne force with a more moderate and rational argument. To them the aeroplane and the parachute were one more way of getting the man to the battlefield. Once there he fought like any other soldier and so, apart from any restrictions imposed by the aerial arrival, his weapons would be the same. By the time the British and Americans started their experiments, the success of the Germans had overclouded the Russian approach, and to some extent both Allied countries tended to look on their airborne weapon needs as being a little out of the ordinary, though not actually so highly specialised as to need special designs.

To make small numbers of special weapons is expensive; it is expensive in money and it is expensive in factory effort. There is rarely much spare effort in wartime and special designs get pushed to the back of the queue while conventional equipment is given priority. This is exactly what happened to the German parachutists' rifle, to the Japanese rifle and light machine-gun, and to the German recoilless gun.

The requirements of a parachutist's weapons are little different from those of a conventional infantryman, except that size and weight become even more important. Size, because he needs to carry his personal weapons with him when jumping – throughout the war the Allied armies wrestled with this problem. The British rifle and Bren gun were long and awkward. Neither could be carried on the man as he parachuted without fear of injury so both had to be lowered on a rope below the jumper. They were a nuisance in the aeroplane, and a nuisance when he made an exit through the door. In the Whitleys they could not be carried at all and had to go into containers. A folding rifle would have been welcomed with open arms, but there was no question of such a thing being made.

The Americans had the same problem but were slightly better off with their parachute, which gave a lower speed of descent. This enabled a man to strap a rifle down one side of his body and to land without too much fear of hurting himself. They also used the short M1 carbine which may have lacked some stopping power, but was handy and straightforward to carry. Browning automatic rifles and other machine-guns came in containers, along with the ammunition. However luck was with the airborne forces of World War II for just before the real concentration of effort on parachute troops was started, a particular type of weapon was developed in most countries and it suited parachutists ideally. It was the sub machine-gun, which appeared in large numbers in all armies from 1941 onwards. It fulfilled all the requirements for an airborne weapon except that of range, for it was restricted to little more than 100yd for accurate and effective fire. It was conveniently small – whatever the nationality of the designer – and gave one man a good rate of fire for a short time and was compact and light.

Weight is important because everything that the parachutist uses has to be flown in to the drop zone, sometimes over several hundred miles of enemy territory and once on the ground it will in all probability have to be carried by marching men rather than in a vehicle. Unfortunately the laws of weaponry usually mean that not much can be cut off the weight of a weapon without some other aspect having to suffer in compensation – generally strength and reliability. So the business of cutting down weight had to be approached with more than usual caution.

Germany

In Germany the airborne forces were fairly well served for their weapons, though it was hardly a bed of roses all the time. Parachute troops were under command of the Luftwaffe, and Goering was the C-in-C. They were therefore his troops, and to some extent he competed with the army. The German airborne were from the first a sort of aerial marine corps, with loyalties to both the army and the air force. Like marines, they were carried to battle by another service, but then fought in conjunction with, and in the same way as, the army. They were also able to exploit both services in getting what they wanted, just as marines have done for hundreds of years. The analogy can be carried further because Goering's airborne lived with the Luftwaffe in the same way as marines live with their navy, and to some extent they shared their duties on the ground. It was natural therefore for them to turn to whichever service would serve them best when it came to equipping themselves. Their best known weapon was the parachutists' rifle, the *Fallschirmjaeger Gewehr* 42. This remarkable weapon was produced entirely for parachute troops, and against the wishes of the army who at the same time were developing a similar rifle with only small differences in the overall performance. However, the parachutists had firm ideas on what they wanted, and the army rifle did not fill the bill. The army was asking for a true assault rifle, but the Luftwaffe felt that it needed rather more than that. The FG 42, as it came to be known, was intended to be a combination of rifle and light machine-gun, capable of being used as either. It weighed 10lb – just right for a rifle – but a bit light for a machine-gun. It took a twenty round magazine – more than enough for a rifle, but perhaps too few for a machine-gun. It had an ingenious mechanism whereby, when single shots were fired by a rifleman, the bolt closed on the next round in the breech and when the trigger was pulled only the light firing pin had to move. This meant that there was the least possible shake immediately before firing, and also that the time between operating the trigger and the actual firing of the cartridge was reduced to the shortest possible. When set to automatic, the trigger mechanism was shifted and the bolt now remained to the rear, leaving the breech open

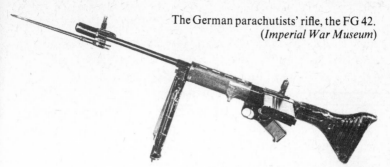

The German parachutists' rifle, the FG 42.
(*Imperial War Museum*)

when the trigger was released so that air could get to the breech and cool it, and so also that a round was not left in a hot breech where it might 'cook off'. This remarkable versatility was copied by the US designers who produced the present M60 machine-gun and it has served well throughout the Vietnam war to the present day.

The FG 42 had a bipod, which folded under the stock, and a small neat spike bayonet clipped under the muzzle. When not in use, it was reversed in its holder and then lay under the barrel, its point safely tucked out of harm's way between the joints of the bipod legs. The magazine fed in from the left – not the best way to do it, but a compromise forced on the designer by the short overall length and the need to bring the breech back as far as possible into the butt in order not to lose barrel length. The sights folded to make a slim outline when the weapon was stowed in a container or carried on the man, and the stock and butt were made either of laminated wood, plastic, or – in a few cases – steel. In every way it was a remarkable gun, although it used no entirely new principles. The prototypes were produced in an almost incredibly short time, and were popular from the start. The difficulty was to find factory capacity to build the rifle, and by the time it had been approved the Crete operation was over and Hitler had decided that he could not afford the casualties of another airborne assault. So the FG 42 never got the use it deserved. It was carried by the men who rescued Mussolini, and was used in the battle of Cassino; thereafter it appeared in small numbers only on the Western Front in the closing days of the war. All told only 7,000 or so were made. Although a brilliant design, the FG 42 failed in two ways. It was too late by one year. Had it been in the hands of the troops at Crete it would undoubtedly have made its name and been given some sort of priority in manufacture. But it missed complete acceptance for another reason: it was too light for the cartridge it fired. The Luftwaffe wanted the full-power 7·92mm round which the bolt-action rifles and proper machine-guns fired. FG 42 represented a tremendous effort to achieve this, and it very nearly did, but it was plagued by continual troubles and was still being modified when the war ended.

The reasoning for asking for the powerful cartridge was that the parachute troops needed the maximum fire power they could possibly get. The standard bolt-action rifle of the German Army was the K 98, the same weapon in 1940 as it had been in 1918, and it has never been noted for rapidity of fire. The machine-gun was the MG 34, a very good gun, but too heavy to be carried on the parachutist so that it would have to be packed into a container – with all the hazards of that means of delivery. It required a crew of two and sometimes three, and the Luftwaffe wanted to increase the fire power of the individual, not the section, although that was obviously intended also. The FG 42 was the right weapon for the job; it made every man a machine-gunner when the occasion demanded, and it was light and small enough to be a personal weapon. At the same time it had the range and penetration of the well-proven 7·92mm cartridge and its ready availability also. The reasons were good; it was the Laws of Physics that were obstructive.

The light weight and powerful cartridge meant that the rifle was difficult to hold steady when firing on automatic, and the spread of the burst was wide. This could undoubtedly have been tolerated because of the resultant increase in fire power, but the working parts were stressed to their limits in coping with power of the round, and had to be made of the best possible materials. They also demanded much machining and skilled fitting, and high-class metal and good machinists were getting scarce in Germany by the time the weapon came into service. Inferior metal gave rise to continual troubles, which were still being sorted out when the war ended. The final blow to the FG 42 was the serious loss of confidence in the value of airborne assaults after the heavy casualties in Crete, and with

German 75mm recoilless gun L-G 40. It stripped down into three loads for parachuting in weapons containers. (*US Army*)

this loss of confidence there went also the drive and energy that had demanded the rifle. The army controlled the supply of raw materials, and they made sure that these went to army projects first.

Another German weapon which was novel and whose use was almost entirely confined to airborne forces was the recoilless gun. There was nothing particularly new in recoilless guns, the principle having been known for some years, but the Germans perfected the idea of using a backward stream of gas to balance the recoil, where other designs had fired a second projectile to the rear. This then was a substantial step forward, and it was developed in great secrecy in the Krupp works. In 1940 they produced their first model, the LG 75mm. LG stood for *Leicht Geschoss* (light gun) and it was truly light. It weighed about 300lb, had a small carriage of motor-cycle wheels, and broke into four loads for parachuting in containers. A few were tried out in Crete and found wanting in some respects. The design was modified and 450 were then produced. The modified gun became the LG 40, and had a sliding block breech and a central percussion primer. This is unusual for

79

recoilless guns, because unless several gas venturis are fitted, the rearward gas flows straight past the firing mechanism and soon wears it out. However, since the gun was cheap, this probably did not weigh too heavily with the manufacturer. At any rate, it was a useful support gun, and fired a high explosive shell weighing 12¼lb to a maximum range of 7,500yd. It was given an anti-tank shell which weighed 10lb, and penetrated an impressive thickness of armour. The production gun ran on a narrow high carriage fitted with two alloy wheels, and when it was fired three legs were let down. Never intended to be towed by a vehicle, the LG 40 was strictly for foot troops, and was assigned to mountain infantry as well as airborne. It was the forerunner of the many recoilless guns which appeared in the next twenty odd years, and it seemed to hit the right design first time. As an artillery piece this Lilliputian Big Bertha has never received the attention that it deserved.

The LG 40 was followed by two other types, few if any of which saw service. The first was the RFK 43, which was an even lighter version of the LG 40. Most of the weight in the LG 40 was contained in the breech mechanism, and the RFK set out to reduce this. It did so by a most unusual system, for this gun broke open at the breech just like a shot gun. The barrel tilted downwards to allow a round to be slipped in, and when it clicked shut, the firing pin was cocked at the same time. This reduced the weight to an incredible 95lb but the range came down also, to just over 2,000yd. Perhaps the loss of range was not so important; the barrels were short, the sights simple, and presumably there was not very much in the way of sophisticated fire-control equipment to calculate ranges and elevations. No doubt most of the shooting was at targets directly in view of the gunners, and a pair of binoculars would suffice to correct shots. The RFK had no wheels, but was carried in separate loads and set down on its legs when needed for firing. As it weighed about the same as the water-cooled Maxim machine-gun, this was not asking too much of the crew, and it fired a high explosive shell of 8½lb.

At the same time as the RFK appeared, a bigger brother of the LG 40 came out as well. This was in 105mm calibre, and was meant to give more substantial fire support in sustained operations. The weight went up to 1,150lb, although it could be taken down very quickly into several one- or two-man loads. The maximum range was over 8,500yd, and the shell weighed 27lb. It fired an anti-tank round and a smoke, both of which ought to have been quite effective. However, the gun does not seem to have been taken into service in any numbers and the LG 43 – as it was termed – was another excellent German idea which was never quite perfected, but which showed others how it ought to be done. Perhaps the LG 43 was going in the wrong direction for the German airborne, as they were organised and equipped, for it was too large for man-handling over more than short distances, yet the Germans had no suitable vehicles in their airborne division to pull it. As the German airborne faded in importance, so their guns seem to have gone also.

Japan

The Japanese Army showed some concern for equipping paratroops and in 1941 various rifles were put under study to determine the best one for air dropping by container. From this study and also from the results of the Sumatra parachute operation it was decided that a special rifle would be needed. In fact the final rifle was really only a modified Type 99, altered so that it could be broken down into two sections. The joint was forward of the breech and the barrel section had the last 1¼in of barrel protruding. This plugged into the forward end of the receiver, locked with a half turn and was secured with a captive pin. Early models worked loose at this joint and it became difficult to extract the empty cartridge cases after 2,000 or so rounds, but this was corrected after further research and the rifle was standardised as the Type 2 (Tera) paratroop rifle in May 1943. Rather as with the Germans, the Japanese airborne were almost finished in an airborne role by this late stage of the war, and it is not now clear how many of these specialised rifles were made, nor where and in what numbers they were used.

A requirement for a light machine-gun for parachute use came at the same time as the one for the rifle. Once again the response was along the same lines, and the standard Type 99

LMG was modified by the Nagoya Arsenal to break down into five separate parts. The research for this apparently straightforward variant seems to have taken an unusually long time; the first tests on the gun were not conducted until 1943, after which it was standardised as the Model 99 (Teke) paratrooper light machine-gun and went into service in small numbers. The only version seen by the author was rather looser at the joints than one would normally expect of a machine-gun, but this could now be the result of old age and continual dismantling rather than any specific failing in the design. However, the Type 99 never looked particularly strong even at its best.

The Allies

On the Allied side rather less concern was shown for the needs of the parachutist. All procurement and design of weapons was firmly in the hands of the army in both the USA and Britain, and their over-riding need was to standardise designs and ensure maximum production with as few diversions as possible. So there were no FG 42s or special artillery pieces; however there were some clever adaptions and modifications to existing types, and these had to suffice. Small arms were quite standard, and the carriage of rifles and machine-guns gave rise to several problems. The chapter on containers describes how these were overcome, and will not be repeated here, but sub machine-guns were nearly always carried with the butt removed and the gun stuck into the harness of the parachute on the chest. The US airborne favoured carrying Thompsons behind the reserve parachute, at an angle, while the British pushed their Stens in horizontally. It made little difference. The gun was ready when the man landed, and it was fortunate that both types could be stripped in this way. Several attempts were made however to produce a special paratroopers' sub machine-gun. In 1943 the Mk 4 Sten was made in prototype for this purpose, but it was never built in quantity. A Mk 2 Sten was cut down in length and fitted with a skeleton butt which folded underneath the gun so that the general outline resembled a large pistol. With the butt unfolded it was a sub machine-gun. Unfortunately the reduction in length brought about a corresponding reduction in effectiveness and the idea was abandoned. At the same time the BSA company designed a completely new sub machine-gun for airborne troops and called it the Welgun, but it too was never adopted. It was a neat little weapon whose butt folded to allow an over-all length of only 17in. It used a Sten magazine and barrel and weighed 6¼lb. Whether it would have been any great advance on the Sten is now difficult to say, it would probably have been plagued with the same unreliability and its small size would hardly have made up for that. But it was a step in the right direction.

The favourite weapon of the US airborne soldiers was the ·30in M1 carbine. This little rifle was not specifically intended for airborne use, but it was immediately adopted by them and huge numbers were produced by US arms firms. In early 1942 a folding butt was introduced so that it could be carried on a parachutist and not interfere with his landing and by 1945 150,000 of this type had been made. The M1 was a delightful carbine both to carry and to fire. It only weighed 5lb 7oz, yet it could be fitted with a 30-round magazine and was semi-automatic. Later models were capable of firing automatic also, though the weapon was so light that on auto it could scarcely be held on the target. The only drawback to the M1 was its lightweight bullet which limited its effective range to little more than a couple of hundred yards, but not many troops worried about that.

The idea of converting ordinary infantry rifles to special airborne versions by folding the butt quickly caught on in other countries and in post-war years both the French and Italian armies adopted the principle. The French put a folding skeleton butt onto the MAS 36 rifle, and in Italy the Beretta BM 59 is produced in a *Paracuditisti* model.

The British Commandos and airborne troops did make one special weapon of their own, though it was hardly a significant one. In the early days of World War II the grenades available to the infantry were very little better than improved versions of World War I types. These were not always well suited to the peculiar sort of warfare being practised by the unconventional forces, and it was not long before private versions began to

Men of the 505th Regiment demonstrating their Bazooka. They were the first formation to be equipped with this weapon. Oujda, North Africa, 1943. The man on the left is carrying an ·30 M1 carbine fitted with a folding butt. (*US Army*)

appear. The Gammon grenade, as it was called after its inventor, was one of these and it was later dignified by being given the number 86. It was a cloth bag with a percussion fuze in the mouth; the thrower filled the bag with sufficient explosive for the job in hand, took off the safety cap, and threw. A short safety tape unwound and after that when the grenade struck anything it went off. The charm of the idea lay in the choice offered to the thrower. The danger lay in the amount of explosive that the bag would carry, and the short length of the safety tape. A reluctant Ordnance Board accepted the design with several provisos in 1943, but later insisted that the safety tape was lengthened to prevent premature explosions. The main use for this grenade was meant to be for anti-tank defence, a pound or so of explosive against the armour of a 1941 tank did a good deal of damage, but the Gammon had plenty of other uses. It made a passable anti-personnel weapon with some scrap metal packed round the explosive, and regimental enthusiasts were able to let off a certain amount of steam by inventing local variations. It was carried by the 1st Parachute Brigade in North Africa in 1941 and was successfully used.

The only other British infantry weapon to be specifically modified for airborne use was the humble 2in mortar, the platoon artillery, with a range of 500yd. The barrel of this was cut down in length from 21in to 14, the base plate altered, and the overall weight reduced from 19lb to just over 10lb. It was no great war-winning weapon, but it served well in several airborne campaigns and is still in service – looking much the same as it did in 1943. Other mortars were treated in the same way to cut down their size and bulk for easier loading and carrying. The US Army produced a cut-down 81mm mortar mainly for jungle use, but it was also adopted by the airborne. The weight was reduced by almost exactly half to just over 66lb, but the range came down by the same proportion, giving a little over 2,000yd at best with a light bomb. This was enough for most purposes, and certainly better value for weight than trying to carry the full-size mortar. The same idea of cutting the barrel length and lightening the mount was followed by both Germany and Japan, but in small numbers, and obviously not too enthusiastically. Neither had the factory effort to spare for special models, and in both countries the airborne arm was hardly used in its special role after 1942.

In Britain, as the war progressed and the number of gliders increased, more thought was given to the problem of delivering immediate fire support to the troops on the ground, particularly when they were out of range of fighter cover and friendly artillery – just the situation that had occurred in North Africa. Although the 25-pounder was an excellent gun, it weighed nearly two tons, and to carry it in a glider involved major modifications to the gun. These were finally achieved and resulted in the so-called Mark 3 carriage which was a combination of the narrow axle produced in India, and a folding

Men of the 1st Airborne Division firing the 75mm airborne howitzer. (*Imperial War Museum*)

trail which originated in Canada: truly an Empire gun, and one which survived for some years after the war in airborne forces. But the weapon most frequently used was the American 75mm pack howitzer. This popular little gun was developed before the war for animal transport in mountain country. It had a short barrel, pneumatic-tyred wheels, a folding box trail, and it broke down into nine loads for parachuting. It was strong and simple, both excellent military virtues, and it threw a 10lb shell to over 7,000yd. For conventional artillerymen this was a miserably short range, but for airborne troops with nothing else it was just about miraculous. It was delivered both by parachute and by glider – more usually the latter because the gun could be brought into action more quickly from a glider; its ammunition could be alongside it, and with the Horsa glider its towing jeep could be carried in the same aircraft. The little 75 remained in service on both sides of the Atlantic until the late 1950s, and was only handed in with great reluctance when the time came to replace it with more modern guns. It was light, versatile, and forgiving. It is remembered today with much affection by those who have used it, and there is a charming story of an American unit in the Panama Canal Zone who, only two years ago, found two guns and some ammunition in a local ordnance dump where they had been for over a decade. They turned out their old soldiers to fire off the entire stock with huge delight. A few 75s can still be seen in US Army barracks, where they are used as saluting cannon.

4 Transport Aircraft

A parachute force is only as mobile as its aircraft and more than one country found that it was easier to find and train paratroops than it was to build and maintain the aircraft for them. In almost every case, the idea for the airborne force came first and the means to fly it was worked out later.

Germany

The Germans were luckier than anyone else in this respect because they had the good fortune to start their planning with an effective and large transport air fleet already in being. Throughout the 1920s Germany had maintained a close liaison with the Soviet Air Force – training her pilots and aircrews in Russia and watching the developments of new thoughts and techniques. Germany was, therefore, well aware of the potential value of airborne forces long before any of the other West European countries realised it; and her military planners took care to specify that the airliners built for the civilian Lufthansa fleet were capable of being converted to military use with little or no modification.

The mainstay of the Lufthansa was the three-engined Junkers 52/3m and 231 had been delivered by 1934. This ugly and ungainly looking machine with its corrugated surfaces, fixed undercarriage and square-cut wings ultimately proved to be one of the great aeroplanes of the century. It was enormously strong, simple to maintain, and could be operated from fields, roads or grass airstrips. Cargo was loaded through a door in the port side, and additional freight could be carried on bomb racks under the wings and fuselage. Alternatively these points could be loaded with weapon containers for parachute troops.

The Junkers was the ideal machine for the new airborne force and one might almost say that it was tailor made for them. Most versions were powered by three BMW radial engines of 830hp each. This engine was not particularly efficient, nor was its power-to-weight ratio as high as other engines of

A Junkers 52 dropping a stick of parachutists. (*Imperial War Museum*)

similar size, but it was unsophisticated and reliable, and it would work well under appalling conditions and not demand an excessive amount of maintenance. The three engines allowed a useful power output with some degree of safety from one engine failure, and it fitted the prevailing design outlook of the times, for many of the successful long range commercial air liners of the late 1920s had had three engines. Full-span flaps were an innovation and provided greater flexibility in choice of runway and length of take-off and landing run. It could carry eighteen troops, or 10,000lb of freight, or thirteen parachutists over a distance of 700 miles.

Fewer parachutists than passengers were carried in order to allow sufficient space for them to stand up and move about before jumping. The door was low and necessitated a crouching exit in order to get through it, followed by the forward dive which was the mark of the German *Fallschirmjaeger*.

The cargo space was 590cu ft, which was not generous, but it permitted a wide variety of loads to be carried and gave enough room for the parachutists to sit on canvas seats, though they were rather cramped. The whole airframe was of steel tube covered in the well-known corrugated aluminium. This was remarkably resistant to damage and generally tough, but from inside it was noisy to a degree in the military version, and it is hard to imagine that the civil passenger planes were much quieter.

A further 450 Junkers were made for the Luftwaffe in 1934 and 1935 though the Luftwaffe was still officially not in existence when the first ones were delivered. More were produced in the following years, but the initial production meant that the Luftwaffe could call upon more than 600 transport planes – theoretically capable of carrying 7,800 parachutists – before any airborne forces were formed in Germany at all. This is an exaggerated picture, because not all the planes would have been available at one time, nor would their crews have been specially trained, but the machines were built and were flying, at a time when there were virtually none in other countries.

For parachuting, the cargo compartment was stripped bare except for the canvas seats and a strong point for the static lines was fitted. A hooter was put in to give the jump signal, and that was all. It was very basic, but there was little to go wrong, and the same general layout was still being used successfully in the Spanish Military Parachute School which was operating Ju-52s as late as 1963. The only change in this case was that the number of parachutists carried had been decreased to ten, which may have been in deference to the age of the aircraft.

Ju-52

The Ju-52 was the workhorse of the Luftwaffe. It appeared on every battle front, and flew throughout the war. In Russia it was the standard supply aircraft and cargo carrier and flew in all weathers. Many were fitted with skis in winter and the great majority had an open machine-gun position just behind the pilot's cabin which gave some defensive capability. In the battle of Crete 170 were lost; many others were shot down over the Mediterranean while taking reinforcements and supplies to North Africa. The last time that the Junkers was used in the parachute role was in the early morning of Sunday 17 December 1944, when 100 weary Ju-52s took off from Lippspringe and Paderborn carrying Colonel von der Heydte's scratch parachute force, destined for the Ardennes. Only ten or twelve aircraft found the dropping zone; the remainder bun-

A Transall of the modern Luftwaffe delivering a load by ULLAD (Ultra Low Level Aerial Delivery.)

dled out their unfortunate passengers to drop anywhere that they could, and very many were injured in the landing. It was not a happy finale. From then on they were purely transport aircraft, and they never again carried parachutists on operational flights. The marriage between the German airborne and the Junkers which helped to make that force lasted seven years, the entire span of the active life of the parachutists. The Junkers, however, lived on. By 1943 it was already outdated, a clear anachronism in an age of retracting undercarriages, longer ranges, higher speeds and heavier loads. But it survived because it was there, and it was rugged, simple and reliable. It was still flying when the war ended. Few machines have had such an epitaph.

There was a strong need for an aeroplane with better cross-country and small-field capability, and to meet this the Arado 232 was developed. This was a high-winged monoplane with a bulbous fuselage and a high-set single boom to the tail. It was powered by four radial engines, and all told looked very much like a smaller version of the British Beverley which appeared in the 1950s. There was a tail loading door, twin fins and rudders, and the same rounded nose. An unusual point was the landing gear, which consisted of a normal tricycle layout backed up by twenty smaller wheels arranged in two rows under the fuselage. With these it could land and take off from rough and unprepared strips, as well as roll over ditches of up to 5ft width. In the event only ten or twelve were made and it never got beyond the experimental stage.

Junkers 252CW

This aircraft was again a three-engined all-metal transport. It differed from the Ju-52 in having a stressed-skin construction, but was still a conventional two-wheeled undercarriage aeroplane. It carried a winch for lifting heavy loads into the freight compartment, and also had a loading aperture underneath the floor. It was never pursued, and one reason which led to its being abandoned was the fact that it needed over 900yd of hard runway to take off.

Heinkel 111

Despite the comparatively large numbers of Ju-52s in the Luftwaffe, there were never enough for all needs, and the Germans were forced to convert other aircraft for use with airborne forces. In just the same way as the British did, the Luftwaffe took some bombers and carried troops in them. This was not done until the Junkers fleet had been so reduced by battle losses that there were no longer enough of them to cope with the demands, which state of affairs arrived in late 1942. By this time the Heinkel 111 bomber was fast becoming obsolete and Germany was no longer carrying out massive bomber attacks – rather the reverse was happening in fact, she was being bombed herself, and the Heinkel no longer had the range or bomb load to be effective. It was frequently used to drop supplies in containers, and could carry up to nine containers each weighing 550lb. The excellent flight characteristics of the Heinkel led to its being used for parachuting, and in this role it was quite effective. The side door, which the original civilian version had, was not suitable for parachuting as it was too close to the tail for safety. A sliding door was therefore fitted into the belly blister, which normally held an air gunner, and a

The six-engined powered version of the Me-321 glider loading an 88mm gun and towing vehicle. (*Imperial War Museum*)

short chute or slide led down to it. In effect this was the same arrangement as was used in the Hudson by the British. It also towed freight-carrying DFS-230 gliders, though not to any great extent.

The most remarkable use of the Heinkel was in its bizarre appearance as a 'Siamese twin' in a version to pull the giant Me-321 glider. During the development of the 321 it was soon found that the triple-tow, or 'troika', of three Me-110 fighters was highly dangerous and required skilful pilots. General Udet suggested to Ernst Heinkel that a doubled-up He-111 might do the job. From this suggestion sprang what must be the most extraordinary aeroplane of an aviation industry which produced quite a range of oddities. Heinkel took two He-111 H-6 fuselages, complete with their wings and engines, and joined them together at the wing roots. A new centre section was added to make up for the lost outer wing from each plane, and an extra engine put in the middle of it. The total horsepower available was 5,360. There were thus no less than five engines, two fuselages, two sets of undercarriages, two separate tail assemblies and, of course, two pilots. This remarkable machine was flown from the port cockpit, with the second pilot seated about 40ft away in the starboard fuselage

The extraordinary Heinkel 111-Z, the Zwillig. Here seen on an aerodrome in Russia, winter 1943. (*William Green*)

where he had no dual throttles, though he could fly the aircraft through duplicated flying controls and instruments. Understandably such an aeroplane was not easy to fly, but it was powerful enough for the task of towing the 321, and altogether twelve were built and delivered by the spring of 1942.

The Heinkels were absorbed into two of the special Giant Glider Squadrons (*Grossraum-Lastensegelergruppe*), and continued in operation until the last of the squadrons was disbanded in the autumn of 1944, by when only four remained. Throughout their life the Heinkels gave very little trouble and flew hundreds of supply missions in various parts of Russia, towing either the 321 or a pair of Go-242s. Towing speed was in the region of 140mph and there was sufficient fuel for 6hr at maximum power.

When taking off with maximum load in the glider, rockets could be fitted which gave a total thrust of 8,800lb to the tug. However, this was not always possible to do, particularly in the front-line aerodromes in Russia, and the tug and glider combination then needed a good length of runway to get airborne.

Other aircraft types

The four-engined Junkers 90 and the Focke-Wulf 200 were also used by airborne forces at one time or another. Neither was made in large quantities, and both were ill suited to parachuting, but they could carry large loads in the air-landed role,

94

Heinkel He-111 'Zwillig' towing a Messerschmitt Me-321 glider.

and were used for this in the Norwegian Campaign. These large transports were much better suited to straightforward freight carrying to and from proper airfields, and in this role they remained for the rest of the war. Gliders were towed by almost any plane that was powerful enough and was available; so it was for the British. Since the Ju-52 was such a valuable load carrier it was not economic to use it to pull a glider that carried a smaller load than its tug. The same problem faced the Americans, and the Germans attempted to solve it by using obsolete bombers. Two which were pressed into service were the Henschel 126 and the Junkers 87 dive bomber. The latter is somewhat of a surprise at first glance, but it sufficed. It was a relatively slow flier, it had a powerful engine, and after 1942 it was used less and less in its original role. It had no value as a load carrier except for occasional high-density loads such as ammunition, slung between the undercarriage legs, but as a tug it was of use. One other point in its favour was that squadrons of Stukas had been allotted to the airborne divisions as integral bomber support; they therefore were more easily available and their pilots had some idea of the techniques involved. When Rommel was being squeezed out of Tunisia by the 1st and 8th Armies some of his air-transported resupply and reinforcement came in gliders towed by Stukas.

Great Britain

The British started in a more haphazard way. When Winston Churchill sent his now famous minute to his Chiefs of Staff in June 1940, demanding a force of 5,000 parachute troops at the earliest opportunity, he unfortunately neglected to order the aircraft for them at the same time. Whether this would have made a great deal of difference is now hard to say because in the middle of 1940 there were virtually no aircraft in England which were by any standards suitable for military parachuting, and two months later the Air Ministry gloomily reported that they could see no chance of getting any either. They then went on to add that they disagreed with the idea of using the Douglas DC-3 as it was unarmed, and recommended instead that gliders were best towed by bombers, since these could offer some defence from fighter attack by using their gun turrets. The Ministry went on to say that any parachute dropping would have to be an alternative task for heavy-bomber squadrons, but within the Air Ministry they could see little future for the parachute soldier. The outcome of this not altogether helpful attitude was the loan of six Whitley bombers to the Parachute School at Ringway.

The Whitley

The offer of the Whitleys was not quite as generous as it might have seemed because they were already almost obsolete for their original job; but they did have some characteristics which made them reasonably suitable for parachuting. They could fly slowly and they had a long rectangular fuselage with a flat floor. Unfortunately that fuselage was also dark, draughty, cold and uncomfortable. It was difficult to get into and difficult to get out of, and the Whitley started a well-known theory in British airborne forces that the flight to the dropping zone was made deliberately unpleasant in order that there would be no hesitation when the order to jump was given. There were no seats in the Whitley and the stick of ten men sat on the floor

A stick of ten men and their despatcher inside the fuselage of a Whitley. The nearest man has a Mk 2 Sten gun under his harness. All are wearing the early pattern long-sleeved jumping smock and their helmets have the leather chinstrap. About 1941. (*Imperial War Museum*)

with their backs against the wall and their legs outstretched across the width of the fuselage.

On long flights cramp occurred quite often, and in an effort to combat the piercing cold a special sleeping bag was produced. This curious piece of equipment was specially designed to cover a full-size man sitting down whilst wearing a parachute on his back. The lower half looked just like an ordinary sleeping bag which laced up with quick-release cord loops. The upper half was made with two enormous flaps shaped like bat wings. These covered the top part of the man's body and he wrapped them around his parachute and himself. When the time came to get ready to jump the whole bag could be quickly and easily thrown off and left in the plane. Many thousands must have been made because they continued to appear in the quartermasters' stores of parachute battalions for years after the war, where they were often issued as normal sleeping bags. Few soldiers of the later generations realised the original reason for the strange shape of his sleeping equipment, and they are now almost collectors' items.

Whitleys dropping at Ringway, 1941. (*Imperial War Museum*)

Jumping from the Whitley was a nerve-wracking experience. There was no door, and the only way for parachutists to leave the plane was through the hole in the floor which was provided in every Whitley for the fitting of the ventral turret, more usually known by the homely name of the 'dustbin'. This hole was 30in across and 3ft deep: it was in fact a short cylinder let into the fuselage, and it just permitted a parachutist to drop through, provided that he kept his arms rigidly to his sides and his body upright. Any faltering or hunching of the spine meant that either his front or his back hit the side of the cylinder and in either case the result was the same – a severe blow on the face – known as 'ringing the bell'. It was probably the most difficult parachute exit that has been devised so far. For nervous or awkward recruits it was a nightmare. It undoubtedly was directly responsible for many good and otherwise highly motivated men failing to qualify as parachutists and, for those who survived, it frequently built up a dread of the straightforward operation of jumping which took a great deal of time to lose. The impression of one trainee parachutist written at the time makes interesting reading.

As a parachuting aircraft, the Whitley was uncomfortable and highly uneconomical. Inside the low, narrow fuselage ten parachutists sat on the cold, corrugated floor – five forward of the jumping hole and five aft. The slack of their strops – connecting the static lines of their parachutes to the aircraft – were press-studded to canvas panels on the sides of the fuselage.

There was little to look at inside the dimly lit fuselage except the greenish face of the man opposite. For anyone as consistently airsick as I was, the Whitley on a bumpy day was the bitter end.

Few parachutists liked dropping from aft of the hole, because from this side the jumper's feet were blasted rearwards as they emerged into the slipstream. His head consequently pivoted forward, and bloody and broken noses were the result of striking your face against the forward edge of the hole. The idea was to tip your head well back on exit to avoid this, but in the general rush to get out it did not always happen.

The ten men were carried in two batches of five, one five forward of the hole and one aft. When jumping the 'sticks' shuffled towards the hole swinging their legs over the aperture and taking it in turns to jump, one facing forward and the alternate one aft. The equipment containers for the stick were dropped by the half-way man, who paused in his departure to shout 'Container! Container!', threw over a release switch set into the fuselage side, and then jumped himself. The idea of shouting the word 'container' was two-fold. Firstly, it reminded him of what he had to do, and secondly, it allowed sufficient time for the men in the front part of the stick to get clear before the containers fell off the bomb racks. The same technique was carried over to the DC-3 when it came into British service, and the difficulty in this aircraft was to be able to stop the stick of men for long enough to call out the required 'password'. Once a stick of parachutists starts moving towards the door it takes more than one man to stop it for even an instant.

The Whitley jump lights were high up on the port fuselage wall, and the tale is told of a stick of Polish recruits who were flying to Ringway on a sunny day when the inexperienced leader looked up and saw that the red light was lit up. Instantly he scrambled his stick up to the hole and they sat gazing at the red bulb, which was in fact lit by a shaft of daylight coming through the hole, but in the excitement and the gloom this was unnoticed. The plane swayed a little and the green light glowed. With no further hesitation ten ardent Poles launched themselves into the sky over the middle of Manchester and caused a major traffic dislocation as they landed in the streets. None was hurt, which seems to point to a moral somewhere.

The unfortunate Whitley added to its unpopularity by being used for the first British parachute raid of the war, Operation Colossus, the blowing up of two aqueducts in southern Italy. All the parachutists were captured and, although the aqueducts were destroyed, the operation was never considered a success. In some curious way the Whitley, which had flown the raiders to complete satisfaction, was damned along with anything else that could be found as a scapegoat.

Other aircraft types

The Whitley was replaced by the Dakota, and since this was an American plane it will be described later. However, there were others allotted to airborne forces in the efforts of the RAF to make up for the deficit in transport aircraft, and by 1943 there were several types of bomber which were available. One was the Albemarle, designed as a medium bomber and delivered to the RAF in January 1943. It was not a success for a variety of reasons, and its specification was out of date by the time it appeared. It was therefore given to airborne forces and immediately played an important part in the training of parachutists and glider pilots. It was by no means an ideal parachute plane being small, cramped and, like the Whitley, cold. It could carry a load far in excess of the weight of the ten parachutists who could pack into its small fuselage, and so was grossly uneconomical, but it was available. The exit was through a hole in the floor, but it was a large hole which made it easy to jump through, and offered no chance of damaging the parachutist. It was, therefore, quite popular, but it faded from the parachuting scene as the Dakota became available in larger numbers and it was used more and more for glider-towing.

The first Halifax replaced the Mk 5 Whitley in 295 Squadron early in 1943, and was used exclusively for airborne forces from then on. From time to time other Halifaxes from other RAF squadrons were borrowed, and a variety of different versions were employed, but the mainstay came from the Mk 5s of 295. Being a bomber, the Halifax was hardly the most suitable machine, but it was the only aircraft that was in service with airborne forces which could tow a Hamilcar glider, and with this the radius of action was 400 miles. With a Horsa it was 600 miles, and most of the Horsas that went to North Africa went there behind a Halifax. They had a long and harrowing journey around France and over the Bay of Biscay, but all except three of them reached the final destination, a tribute not only to the aircraft but also to the determination and grit of the glider pilots who flew their awkward and heavy machines for wearying hours on the end of a tow line.

As a parachuting aeroplane, the Halifax was very uneconomic because, for all its size, it too could fit only ten men into the fuselage. They jumped through a hole in the floor which was comfortably large, but which the wags were quick to point out closely resembled a coffin in size and shape. Coffin-shaped or not, the 'Halibag' was always reckoned to be a good plane to jump from, but it was used only for training.

The Short Stirling was another RAF bomber which was getting elderly by the end of 1943 and no longer needed for night operations, with the result that many were transferred to 38 Group early in 1944. It remained in production, however, and the later versions were fitted with a glider tow hook in the assembly factory. Gradually the Albemarles were replaced by the Stirlings, until by 1945 six squadrons had been equipped. The Stirling was a good glider tug with a radius of action similar to the Halifax although it was not used for the Hamilcar. It could carry twenty-two paratroops who jumped through a hole in the rear of the fuselage, but again it was an expensive way of flying them and not many were so used; glider towing was its main task.

At least ten other types of aircraft were used by British airborne forces at one time or other during the war. Some only appeared briefly on the airborne scene, – like the Hurricane which was used on a few occasions to drop supplies from its wing pylons. Others, such as the Hawker Hart put in thousands of hours of flying, towing Hotspur gliders in 1941 and 1942. The Audax did the same, together with the Hector and the Miles Master. Indian airborne forces used the Lockheed Hudson for training and for some minor operational jumps. An odd feature of the Hudson was that the exit was down a plywood chute and out through the floor. The fuselage was small in cross section with a tiny door and had no convenient hole in the floor as had the big bombers. An aperture was cut near the tail, where it did not weaken the structure, but there was no easy way for a man wearing a parachute to get to it and make a proper exit. The Parachute Training School at Ringway produced the chute, each man lying down on it and sliding out feet first into the slipstream in what has been described as the most enjoyable way of leaving an aeroplane that has ever been devised.

The USA

The aircraft used by US airborne forces constitute little more than an account of that incredible machine, the C-47 Dakota.

The Dakota

There used to be a saying that the three weapons that won World War II were the Dakota, the Liberty ship, and the Jeep. It is certainly true to say that without the Dakota the Allied airborne operations of 1944 and 1945 would have been impossible, and so would many other military efforts. The machine that started its life as a luxury sleeper-berth airliner in 1936 became the workhorse of the Allies and the mainstay of their armies.

When the USA came into the war there were nearly 300 DC-3s in regular air-line service in the country, and already some were in military use. This model was not well suited for use as a military transport, having been designed for purely civil operations. Many of those taken over were flown with their civilian interiors unaltered and were used as staff transports. A very small number was bought by the British Pur-

A C-47 Dakota snatching a glider. Upottery, Somerset. March 1944. (*US Army*)

chasing Commission and shipped to the Middle East and India, but before any substantial quantities could be delivered the Japanese struck at Pearl Harbour.

Luckily most of the design work required to make the DC-3 into a proper military transport had already been done long before the USA entered the war, and the first orders for the C-47, or Dakota as the RAF called it, had been placed in 1940. These first versions were known as the C-53 or Skytrooper and appeared in October of 1941. In January 1942 came the C-47 Skytrain, the first of a long line from which over 2,000 were delivered to the RAF alone. The general features of the Dakota are so well known to any person with the slightest interest in aviation that they will not need to be repeated here, but it may be apposite to remind other readers that it is a twin-engined, low-wing monoplane with radial engines and a wing and fuselage built with a partially stressed aluminium skin. It was essentially simple and robust, yet it was at the same time years ahead of its German counterpart, the Junkers. As a troop carrier it lifts twenty-eight men; as a cargo carrier it will take

7,500lb to a maximum range of 1,500 miles (it should be noted that this description is couched in the present tense because this remarkable aeroplane is still in military service in many parts of the world). In the parachute role twenty fully equipped men are carried, the reduced numbers being caused by the extra weight of a man with a parachute on his back, and the greatly increased space that such a man needs. The parachute exit is through a door on the port side just forward of the tail, and static lines are clipped either to an overhead wire or one which runs along the starboard side above the seats. The normal cruise speed varies according to the type and engines fitted, but it lies within a band from 180mph to 200mph. For parachuting, the dropping speed is below 100mph, and an experienced pilot can fly in at just over 85mph with both engines throttled back and the plane slowly losing height as it crosses the dropping zone. At this speed the slipstream offers little if any resistance to a man stepping out of the door, and an easy exit is followed by a sensation of riding down a long slope while the parachute is pulled out and deployed from behind. It is a most forgiving plane to jump from, and errors can be made in the door which will bring instant retribution in the form of twists in the rigging line or somersaults if attempted from faster machines.

The USAAF rapidly equipped its transport groups with the C-47 during 1941 and 1942. Four such groups arrived in England in the summer of 1942, bringing more than 200 C-47s with them, and more came in the following winter. However, it was not until September 1943 that No 1 Parachute School at Ringway was able to borrow any of the new machines in order to train students in the technique of jumping through a door, and the 1st Parachute Brigade carried out their operations in North Africa using C-47s of the USAAF with the absolute minimum of training in the use of the plane. As a result, there were more injuries than would have been expected, and when this fact was realised the school was given more aircraft. The US Army had been fortunate enough to have the C-47 on hand when its airborne forces began, and so was in roughly the same satisfactory position as the Germans. In point of fact this statement is only partly true, for parachute training started before the C-47 proper appeared, and early jumps were from converted B-18 bombers and DC-3s. But when the great expansion in the US airborne forces came about in late 1941 and 1942 there were enough C-47s to lift not only the paratroopers but the air-landed forces as well. The US paratrooper of World War II had to learn only one set of aircraft drills and one jump technique; for him an airplane was a C-47. It helped a lot.

Despite its many obvious virtues there were some drawbacks to the C-47, and these became particularly noticeable when using the machine as a military transport. The floor is a long way from the ground, and much too high for an ordinary truck to discharge its load straight through the door. The same floor is not particularly wide, and it was a stroke of luck that jeeps and anti-tank guns fitted it with sufficient space to allow them to be brought in through the door. Loading these equipments was by no means easy, however. They had to be pushed or, in the case of the jeep, driven, up a steep ramp, joggled round the corner at the top, and heaved up the fuselage, all against gravity. They could then be lashed down, leaving very little space for the crew to slither round or over them as they passed up and down. Such a loading manoeuvre took time to complete, in sharp contrast to the rapid methods with today's tail-loading planes. Unloading was a little quicker, but all the time care had to be taken not to let gravity take control, and getting an anti-tank gun onto the ground could be expensive in grazed fingers.

The C-47 continued in service with the US airborne forces until replaced by the C-119 in the early 1950s, and it was phased out of British airborne service in the same time frame, making way for the Valetta and the Hastings. The Valetta was one of many aircraft which have appeared in post-war years as 'Dakota replacements', but nothing seems to satisfactorily replace this incredible machine and it continues to fly in all parts of the world, having not only outlived its rivals but most of its intended replacements, as well.

Other aircraft types

One machine which the US airborne used in small numbers in the latter stages of the war was the Curtiss C-46 Commando.

This was a bigger plane than the C-47, with a distinctive 'double bubble' fuselage. It was first used operationally in the Rhine crossing when seventy-two of them lifted the 513th Parachute Regiment onto a drop zone near Hamminkeln. Sadly, there was a peculiarity about the C-46 which caused it to catch fire easily when hit by flak, and twenty-four of the 513th's were shot down in flames that day, although the parachutists jumped out of all but one. If a wing tank was punctured the fuel ran down into the fuselage, and another strike would set the plane ablaze in a second. General Ridgway refused to let it be used in Europe again, but thirteen of them took part in the recapture of the Philippines in June 1945 without incident. The vulnerability of the C-46 ruined it as a military transport, which was a pity because it was both powerful and capacious. It could carry forty troops in the transport role, or thirty paratroopers, but it also came too late to be of any decisive effect – the C-47 had already done the job. There are still some C-46s earning their living as freight carriers in various parts of the world, but they are becoming rare and the US Airborne Museum at Fort Bragg has felt it worthwhile putting one outside their building in its wartime camouflage.

Russia

Before the war the Soviet airborne forces had very few aircraft actually assigned to them for their exclusive use. There were some military transport planes, and these were used by those branches of the service which had most need of them at the time.

The ANT-6

The fleet was pretty mixed but the only machine of significance to airborne troops was the ANT-6. This has been mentioned before in this book; it was a four-engined mid-winged monoplane of a design reaching back to the late 1920s. The undercarriage was fixed and had two main wheels, so that the fuselage sat on the ground at a steep angle making it difficult to load cargo into the hold. The maximum load was about 5 tons, depending on the fuel carried. In the troop-carrying role twenty-five to thirty parachutists could be flown over a com-

A C-46 Commando loading up before the Rhine crossing, May 1945.

bat radius of 250 miles. The flying speed was low and the dropping speed could be brought down to little more than 70mph. It was powered by four liquid-cooled motors, cowled into an enormous wing covered with corrugated metal cladding. A version of this machine was flown to the North Pole in the late 1930s and contemporary newspapers published photographs of Soviet scientists standing on the ice in the shelter of the huge wings.

This venerable machine was obsolete well before the war started but it remained in service until the last one wasted out from battle damage and old age some time after 1942. It was replaced by the Soviet version of the Douglas DC-3.

The Dakota in Russia

Licence production of the DC-3 was started in 1939 and the first civil models went into service in 1940. In 1941 all were mobilised, and manufacture accelerated. In addition, the USA supplied more ready-built C-47s and by the end of the war there were over 2,000 DC-3 type of aircraft flying in the Soviet Union. These were the machines which formed the backbone of the air-transport fleet of the Soviet airborne forces through the war. They carried the freight, pulled the gliders and dropped the parachutists, just as they did for the Allies in all the other war zones throughout the world. Many are still flying.

The Soviet version of the DC-3 was known as the Li-2. The designer of the 'Sovietised' DC-3 was Boris Lisunov, who made certain modifications to the original version to enable it to be made in factories in the USSR. The external differences were scarcely noticeable, and the differences in performance and load carrying, negligible. Despite the appalling climate and primitive airfields, the Li-2 was an enormous success.

The Ilyushin Il-12

The replacement after the war was the Ilyushin Il-12, a plane whose design had begun in 1943. The Il-12 was slightly larger than the Li-2, carried about six more men, and was both more powerful and faster. It went into military service in 1948 and remained in use until the end of the 1950s. It lacked the simplicity and robustness of the DC-3, but even so it was much tougher than its equivalents in Western countries. The cargo hold was not much larger than the DC-3 and the payload was only a little better. However, its tricycle undercarriage made loading and unloading much easier.

These two planes provided the air lift of the Soviet airborne forces for the first ten years of the post-war period, and then there was a surprising and sudden change.

The Antonovs

At the 1956 Tushino Air Display an entirely new twin-engined transport plane was flown past the crowd. It had an upswept rear fuselage, a rear loading door, a multi-wheel main undercarriage, a very large wing and two powerful airscrew-turbine engines. It came as a complete surprise to Western observers, and it was obvious that it must be a successful design that was already in production, otherwise it would never have been exhibited. In military service the payload was about 9 tons or forty-five to fifty parachutists. It was an Antonov design, the An-8, and it remained in use for more than ten years. The An-8 heralded the change in Soviet heavy-dropping practice, for this was the first Soviet machine that could open its rear doors and drop a skid-board over the sill. It was steadily developed.

The next Antonov design was the An-10 which came out in 1957. It was an enlarged An-8 with four engines but no rear loading doors and hence could only be used for passengers and cargo. However it was a most successful civil plane and from it was developed the military version, the An-12. In effect this was an An-10 with an upswept rear fuselage and rear doors. A gun turret was installed at the base of the large single fin and rudder. This machine has been a huge success and has been supplied to all the Eastern Bloc countries as well as being bought commercially by several other countries. It is still in service in large numbers in many parts of the world, including the USSR. The payload is about 20 tons over a range of 650 miles at a cruising speed of 340mph, and in the parachute role 80 fully equipped parachutists can be carried and dropped through the side doors. When heavy loads are dropped, the doors are closed for the approach flight, opened over the drop zone, and closed for the return. The plane is capable of carrying and dropping two ASU-57 SP anti-tank guns on two platforms. The performance and capability is very similar to that of the Lockheed C-130 Hercules, with the exception that the C-130 has a better range. The An-12 has been and still is, the work-horse of the Soviet airborne forces. Its speed, payload, ability to use rough fields, together with a large hold, make it invaluable as a military transport, and it seems likely to continue in service for some years yet.

Japan

Japanese aircraft were almost always far less efficient than their western equivalents, and Topsy is a good example of this failing.

Topsy

Topsy was the Mitsubishi Ki-57 Army Type 100 Transport Model 1 – to give her her full title. There was a Model 2 but it appeared only in small numbers. Topsy originated in early 1939 as a commercial transport and was slightly changed for military use in 1940. Very broadly, Topsy resembled the DC-3, being an entirely conventional low-wing monoplane, with radial engines, a single fin and rudder, and two-wheeled under-carriage. There was plenty of wing area, although all dimensions were about threequarters the size of the DC-3. Thus the wing span was 74ft against 95ft for the DC-3. However, the engines gave almost the same total horsepower and one might have expected a reasonable carrying capability from Topsy. Instead she was most disappointing. The passenger load was eleven with a crew of four (the DC-3 required three), and the cargo payload is quoted as being between 3,000 and 4,000lb. This may well have been the maximum that could be carried, with a consequent reduction of range. The normal operating range was 900 miles, which was adequate, but the DC-3 could fly for 2,000 miles with twice the load.

Topsy's claim to fame was her use for the Japanese air assault and parachute drop on the aerodrome and oil refineries at Palembang in February 1942. There were some eye-witness reports from that action which stated that up to seventeen parachutists were counted jumping from one plane, and it is just possible that more than the standard number could have been crammed in for a short flight. It would have been uncomfortable and cramped inside, and the process of checking parachutes before jumping would have been difficult, but as the men jumped virtually without equipment of any kind it could have been managed.

Other Japanese aircraft

Topsy was virtually the only Japanese-designed plane that could carry and drop parachutists; her counterpart Sally, was a cargo carrier and supply dropper. Sally was the Mitsubishi Ki-21-II Army Bomber Type 97 Model II. She was an excellent bomber and was built in large numbers just before the war and during its early years. There was a transport version in being fairly early on in the life of the design and, when the need for transport aircraft became acute during the middle period of the Pacific war, more and more Sallies were converted from bombing. As a passenger carrier, nine men could be carried with some cargo, much of it hung on the wings; as a pure freight carrier the payload was just over a ton, though this could be increased for short-range operations if there was enough room inside the fuselage.

Glider-towing, what there was of it, was undertaken by Nell, a converted navy bomber. Nell was another Mitsubishi design, the G3M2 Navy Type 96 Attack Bomber Model 21, and she was one of the very few Japanese aircraft with twin fins and rudders. Nell was a versatile machine, and was used for several different kinds of offensive task; she was notable for a remarkably long range, well in excess of 2,000 miles at full load. The fuselage was too small to allow her to be of much value as a transport, but she could tow a glider, and this she did from about 1943 onwards, though the opportunities for operational glider-towing were almost nil.

DC-3s were built in substantial numbers in Japan from 1939 onwards and were known as the Nakajima L2D2 Navy Type O Transport, or Tabby to the Allies. The differences between the American and Japanese versions were negligible, and this led to some tragic recognition mistakes throughout the Pacific area. So far as is known, Tabby was only used as a general transport and cargo carrier, though some were used by the navy for training parachutists. The author has been unable to trace any use of the machine for parachute dropping on operations.

The only other Japanese machine to be used in any significant numbers in support of airborne operations was the Lockheed 14 (Lodestar). Versions were built under licence in Japan, and a variant was designed and produced by Kawasaki with a slightly better performance and capacity than the original model. Both types were used operationally in the Palembang assault, and some reports state that men jumped from them. Japanese records show that the main use of the Lockheed was for pure cargo and passenger carrying, and it may be that the Japanese found that the very small door was a barrier to parachuting in the same way as the Allies did with the Hudson, which was almost the same machine.

5 Gliders

Although the parachute soldier could be landed perfectly well with light equipment by parachute alone, the real problem facing the airborne forces of 1940 and early 1941 was that of getting their heavy weapons and vehicles on to the battlefield. If airborne warfare was even to get beyond the stage of short-lived assaults, it was necessary for the troops to be properly supported on the ground. In the German attacks in Scandinavia and over the Dutch water obstacles the main body of the army had caught up quickly, but this was not a reliable method, and in Holland it had failed to work at all well. Quite obviously it would never be any use to rely on a link-up if there was a large obstacle in between the two forces such as the English Channel, or if the enemy put up a stiff fight on the actual dropping zone. In either of these cases the parachute force would lose its advantages of surprise and would be launched into a battle for survival. Once this happens the parachute force is on the losing side; the opponent has the advantages of mobility and superior fire power, while without vehicles the parachutists are limited to the speed of their marching, and are further hampered by having to carry their weapons and ammunition with them. Once the enemy recovers from his surprise he can surround the parachute-landing area, and set about clearing it at leisure, bringing in whatever forces he needs for the job. This very nearly happened to the British 2nd Parachute Battalion in North Africa in November 1942, and was only avoided by some skilful deception and hard marching. To give a better chance of success a means had to be found of delivering heavy equipment.

In the late 1930s and early 1940s the only way to carry a single large heavy load by air was to put it into a glider and tow it with a sufficiently powerful aeroplane. The theory was well established and for some years before the war the idea was put forward in a variety of forms. The attractions lay in the supposed flexibility of the glider, and its comparative cheapness.

The DFS-230.

It was seen as an aerial counterpart to the homely barge on the river, carrying an enormous load, and towed by a tiny tug with a capacity only a fraction of its follower. Some went further than the single glider, and glider 'trains' were foreseen, with the last one in the line 'slipping' its tow line when over its destination, leaving the others to continue without interruption. Unfortunately, nowhere in the world had anyone actually built a load-carrying glider, so while the ideas were all ready and while the advantages were easily seen, there was no experience and no idea of the difficulties or the costs or the limitations. It is therefore all the more remarkable that it was made to work in so short a time as it was.

Germany

As usual it was the Germans who started first. In 1933 the famous Doctor Lippisch decided to use a glider for high-altitude meteorological research. He chose a glider because he required to carry a heavy payload aloft, but did not wish to go to the expense and trouble of using a large aeroplane to do it. A glider was cheaper and easier to maintain, and in flight, free from vibration, noise, and electrical disturbances.

The military version came to be known as the DFS-230, from the initial letters of the institute which designed it, the Deutsche Forschungsanstalt für Segelflug. It was not a particularly inspired design, being little more than a scaled-up conventional sailplane with a larger and wider fuselage. The latter was made of steel tubing covered in fabric, and could carry two pilots in tandem and eight passengers seated on a bench running down the centre, which they straddled with their legs. The wings were shorter than the civilian type of sailplane, but were still very long and graceful. They were good enough for the glider to be capable of soaring if only lightly laden, but some of their efficiency was lost by struts bracing them to the fuselage on the inboard sections. Later on in the war this efficiency was eroded even further by fitting an open cockpit behind the pilot and equipping it with an MG 15 on a ring mount, which could be fired by number one passenger from a standing position. This gun gave some measure of protection to the glider–tug combination. The empty weight of the whole machine was just under 1 ton, and it carried just over a ton; a very good ratio of payload to empty weight. It could be towed at over 100mph and when released it sank at 240ft per min, which is a remarkably low figure, and betrays its sailplane ancestry straight away. This low sinking speed and flat gliding angle was used to great advantage in the first-ever glider operation in the world, namely the assault on the Belgian fort of Eben Emael. Silence and surprise were vital for this and the similar operations launched at the same time, and silence is not a factor normally present at a parachute landing – usually the reverse, in fact. Another feature which made gliders so useful for the *coup de main* was the fact that they delivered their loads in one place at one time without spreading them over a wide drop zone.

In his book *Airborne to Battle* Maurice Tugwell vividly describes the entire action, using much hitherto unpublished material. The germ of the idea was sown by the German Women's Champion Glider Pilot, Hanna Reitsch, who had told Hitler that in flight a glider is almost silent. From this was evolved the plan to land a force on top of the fort by gliding in from a start

DFS-230 on short rigid tow behind a Heinkel He-111.

point over Germany itself. The DFS-230 was ideal for this task, and on the morning of 10 May 1940 forty-one of them were cast off from their Ju-52 tugs at an altitude of 8,000ft, just inside German territory opposite the Dutch town of Maastricht. The Junkers turned away, and the 230s in four groups sailed quietly and steadily over the sleeping farms and villages of neutral Holland on their 14 mile journey into Belgium. Inside the gliders it was cold and eerie, with little to be seen through the small windows, for it was not yet dawn. Each man had a blanket to wrap around himself and in the morning chill it was needed. From inside the gliders were anything but silent. Even the best of gliders makes a distinctive wind noise, but the large military ones had an orchestra all their own.

The wind eddies and screams around the fuselage and wings, whistles through cracks and holes, and moans and thrums on control cables and undercarriage struts. Canvas flaps against the framework of the sides, the wings creak, and in bumpy weather there is a continual groaning, squeaking and twanging as tensions change and the skeleton flexes. To the 350 men in the 230s on that May morning their gliders probably sounded impossibly loud, although after casting off from their tugs the intensity would have died down somewhat. Their airspeed dropped to half what it had been on tow, and the noise diminished accordingly. At 0520 hours, sighing gently and whistling in low key, the gliders landed on their targets, unseen, unheard, and totally unexpected. A bump, a slithering run of less than 30yd, and the flight was over. Instantly, two doors opened in every machine and the troops rushed out. The first gliders to be used in war had succeeded.

The DFS-230 was also used in Crete, but it was not ideal as for that operation it was so small. It could only really carry men, although the engineers who attacked Eben Emael brought with them their demolition explosive charges which weighed 110lb each and were small enough to be carried through the door and stowed on the floor without too much lashing down. However, anything bigger than an ammunition box was barely possible, and there was no question of carrying support weapons. Added to this was the fact that this small load made the DFS-230 non-cost effective, to use a modern expression. Each glider required a skilled pilot and a tug aircraft. The training of a glider pilot took much time (as the Allies were later to find out), and they were better employed if they could fly big loads. Tugs were equally valuable, and although a single Ju-52 could pull three DFS-230s this was not practical for operations, and it was nearly always one-to-one. True the 230 could be pulled by other machines, such as the HS-126 and the Ju-87 Stuka, but this was mainly for training. So each glider really required one Junkers, and a towing Junkers could only carry a small proportion of its available payload. A Ju-52 in the freight role could lift 10,000lb against the 230's 2,000, so the mathematics made the 230 unattractive except for special cases such as Eben Emael.

The Gotha Go-242

The Germans realised this quicker than anybody and by early 1942 had produced the Gotha Go-242, a twin-boom design and a very different looking machine from the almost elegant

A Gotha 244, the powered version of the 242 glider. (*Imperial War Museum*)

230. The Gotha was entirely functional; built of steel and wood, it was square, ugly, and strong. Its only trouble was that it came too late, for by early 1942 the German airborne story was almost over, and the Gotha was never used in action in the way it had been meant to be. The great majority were used for supply missions, mainly on the Russian Front. The first Gothas to appear were fitted out by the Luftwaffe for special duties and several became mobile tactical-command posts, technical workshops, or field dressing stations. This was an effective way to use them in the highly fluid war that was being fought at that time in Russia. The payload of the Gotha was between 4,000 and 4,400lb, the difference arising from the variations in the power of the many aircraft which towed it. Generally it was towed by Heinkel 111s but when there were not enough of these, other bombers were pressed into service. On occasions Dornier Do-17s and what the German documents call 'Italian Savoyas' towed it.

The Gotha was also tried as a powered glider by fitting two engines, when it was known as the Gotha 244. This was a failure and the machine proved to be very dangerous. Despite protests from the pilots two Ju-52 squadrons were converted to Gotha 244 aircraft in the summer of 1942, but had to be hurriedly given back their Junkers after a few months because the losses in aircraft and men were quite unacceptable. Two Heinkel 111 groups were not so lucky and they had to hold on to their unpopular Gothas. The eventual fate of this unit has not been recorded, but there do not appear to have been any 244s left by the end of the war. The glider survived, however, there being five squadrons in existence in 1945.

The Messerschmitt 321

The final chapter in the German glider story was the giant Messerschmitt 321. This huge machine went to the other extreme in that it was meant to carry 130 troops, or one tank, or up to 20 tons of stores. The original idea had sprung from the plans for the invasion of Britain in 1940 and the glider was designed and the first one built at Leipheim at the end of that year. The first production batch were being flown by the middle of 1941, and four squadrons of six aircraft each were in

117

service before the end of the summer. The difficulty was to find planes to tow the giant. Two Heinkel 111s could manage reasonably well, as could three Me-110. This latter arrangement must have been a sight to see, for the Messerschmitts were arranged in a tandem layout called a 'troika'. The difficulties were enormous so the pilots of all four aircraft had to be highly skilled. The marshalling was complicated; the time taken to warm up engines and position for take off was excessive, and there was no question of continuous take-offs from the same airfield. To some extent this trouble was reduced with two Heinkels, but it was still not the answer, and this was not achieved until the extraordinary Heinkel 111-Z was built. This plane is dealt with in the chapter on aircraft and so will not be enlarged upon here.

At the same time as the experiments with the tow aircraft were going on, an attempt was made to ease the take-off run of the loaded glider by fitting hydrogen peroxide rockets under the wings. There were three sizes, giving a thrust from each of 1,100, 1,650, or 2,215lb. Between three and five were strapped under each wing and the burning time was one minute. Apparently these rockets were quite successful and most dramatic to watch. But tow aircraft were always in short supply and in an effort to ease the problem Willi Messerschmitt fitted engines. In order to get any sort of performance at all, six were needed and even so it was a slow flyer with very limited manoeuvrability. The take-off run when loaded was very long, and the payload was reduced by the weight of the engines, but it was worthwhile because it was still 12 tons, larger than that of any other transport aircraft in the whole of World War II. The pilots needed to be very highly skilled to fly it and it could not be flown on instruments alone, but a number went into service.

Other experiments

Although most of the German gliders were used in supply operations there was continuous experiment to discover more effective ways of using them in the airborne assault. One interesting feature which emerged from flying gliders in bad weather in Russia was the rigid tow. Normally a glider was towed by a cable about 130ft long. In darkness or poor visibility the glider could not see the tug, which is a dangerous situation, for the glider must keep itself either above or below the slipstream, but not in it, and it must keep straight behind the tug and not wander from side to side or the pilot of the tug cannot fly straight either. To overcome this difficulty the Luftwaffe used a rigid tow bar which was only 4m long. How often this extremely short tow bar was used is not recorded, but the 4th Air Fleet operating in Hungary in the winter of 1944–5 quite definitely used it with Dornier Do-17s and Heinkel He-111s.

One other mention must be made of German gliding before passing on, and this concerns a concept of use which was exciting and novel. The Parachute Lehr Battalion under Oberstleutnant von der Heydte experimented with methods for putting gliders into small landing zones and through hostile anti-aircraft fire. Von der Heydte was advised by Hanna Reitsch in these experiments, the second time that this redoubtable woman had had an influence on the airborne scenario. In brief, the method was to dive into the landing zone from a great height and to slow down the speed using special drag parachutes. The gliders were released at anything up to 12,000ft and 20 miles away; they then glided in until they were almost overhead of the landing zone; at this point the nose was put down and the parachute streamed from the tail.

The parachute kept the dive speed down to just over 100mph in a practically vertical drop. At 800ft the pilot pulled out, lowered the flaps, hauled the glider round in a short circuit, and put it down on the ground without further hesitation. All landings were on skids, not wheels, and to shorten the landing run still further some gliders had retro-rockets in the nose. A version of this high-altitude glider assault was used in February 1945 to reinforce Breslau. Breslau was surrounded by the Russians at that time and the one airfield was dominated by anti-aircraft guns of all calibres together with searchlights. Any aircraft approaching the field regardless of whether it tried to glide in from altitude or hedge-hop at ground level was picked up and subjected to continuous heavy fire. The runway was under artillery fire at all times, which made it extremely dangerous to leave an aircraft at a standstill for any length of time. It was decided to fly in a battalion of paratroopers in gliders, and this became the last glider operation undertaken by the German Army. The Kaiser Strasse in the middle of Breslau had been widened and cleared for use as a light-aircraft strip and this was to be the landing zone. In late February the battalion was loaded into DFS-230s and Gotha 242s towed by Heinkel 111s to an altitude of roughly 7,000ft. Released over the middle of Breslau, they descended as fast as they dared into the pall of smoke which hung over the city. Most were detected by the Russian searchlights and fired upon, but all landed safely, and delivered their loads despite the heavy concentration of fire. It was a remarkable demonstration of skill and courage, which sadly for the Germans had little or no effect upon the outcome of the battle since it was obvious that the city was doomed.

Great Britain

The British experimented with a more modest version of the same technique in the spring of 1944. A simple arrester parachute was fitted to the gliders which carried the *coup de main* parties to the Orne bridges. In fact, only one actually used it and then only from 1,000ft, when he found that he was overshooting the target, but the principal difficulty had been that of finding the way in poor visibility. A few tries were made at Netheravon with a dive approach from 5,000 or 6,000ft, pulling out at 200ft. A tail parachute retarded the dive, and the machine was landed as soon as it flattened out. Quite rightly, the performance was regarded as too dangerous, and abandoned. In any case, finding the landing zone from 5,000ft in the dark would have been difficult on a clear night, to say the least, and with a little cloud, some smoke and dust on the ground and a few strange lights it becomes next to impossible. In the event, it was always the combined efforts of the tug and gliders' crews which were needed to fix the release point.

It might be worth digressing for a moment to enlarge on this matter of navigation because it was vital to any glider operation. The arrangement in British gliders was that the navigator of the tug guided the combination to the area of the landing zone. From there on the glider pilot and co-pilot assisted also. The glider cockpit was hooked into the tug's intercom by a telephone wire wound in the tow rope, and so could speak to any member of the tug crew. By the time of the Normandy Invasion the usual system was that three marker points called *A*, *B* and *C* were picked up, and the glider cast off at *C*. These points were some miles apart and as far as possible were easily recognized natural landmarks: the intention was to make the cast-off point quite unambiguous. The combination was fairly ponderous in flight, and there was no question of quick changes of course at the last minute, nor was it really a sound policy to try to come round again for another run in. Everything depended on a straight approach, a cast-off at the right spot, a quick get-away by the tug, and the skill of the glider pilots in making the landing. The glider decided when to release from tow, and this was done by a lever in the cockpit. The release height had been fixed in the planning, and from that point a set course was flown to the landing zone. This last part of the flight was a time of intense concentration for the pilots, and invariably one of apprehension for the passengers. The co-pilot often watched the altimeter calling out the height and looking for the final landmarks as the landing zone came into view. On the approach the flaps came down with a hiss from the air bottles, and a shudder in the framework, then the floor tilted down, the wind note changed and the gliders rushed down out of the sky to bump onto the ground and stop almost immediately. One never got used to the landings; the tensions were always the same.

Historically, the British glider position in 1940 can be easily summed up in a very few words. Only a small number of civilian types existed, none suitable for military uses. By the end of 1940 the Air Ministry and the War Office had agreed to produce four types, curiously with little regard in the specifications for the loads that they would have to carry.

The Hotspur

The first was an eight-seater, later called the Hotspur. About 1,000 were built, the original idea being that it should be an expendable machine which made one operational trip only.

The British ten-man Hotspur glider. (*Imperial War Museum*)

There were other equally odd ideas that soon died with experience. It was thought that gliders could carry bombs and supplement the load of the bomber which would tow them. Another idea was to drop parachutists from gliders, and this one took some time to die; yet another was to tow gliders in trains, one behind the other – and for this the first Hotspurs had tow hooks in the tail as well as the nose. But the main use of the Hotspur was to be for the carriage of eight soldiers, and it was envisaged that the glider would be cast off several miles from the objective and silently run in, in the same way as the Eben Emael *coup de main*. The design required a fairly high standard of aerodynamics, combined with cheapness and simplicity. The General Aircraft Co produced the first prototype Hotspur in just over four months, and it was a delightful little machine very much like a high performance sailplane. Without a load it could be, and was, soared. The top half of the plywood fuselage lifted off like a lid and allowed the passengers to climb in or out. The eight soldiers sat astride a bench facing forward, with small portholes to see out.

Shortly after the first Mk 1s appeared the tactical concept changed and it was decided that the best way to assault by

June 1944. A Horsa which had been loaned to the US Army. The tail of this one disconnected easily and allowed its jeep to run out down the lightweight ramps. (*US Army*)

glider was to be towed almost over the landing zone and approach in a steep dive. This called for almost no gliding qualities, but considerable strength. In the Mk 2 the wingspan was reduced by a quarter and doors were cut in the fuselage instead of the lid; these doors were meant for parachuting, but were never used for it. In fact, the Hotspur was never used for operational flights, and spent its entire life as a trainer. Since it had been designed with some care to have only a very short flying life, the change in its use led to further troubles. However, it is remembered with enormous affection by the early generation of pilots and it possessed the priceless feature that it could be towed by comparatively small single-engined aircraft. There were plenty of these in 1940, but very few more powerful machines. So the Hotspur filled a large gap, and did it for over two years.

The Horsa

The second type became the highly successful Horsa, but in case it failed the third specification called for a fifteen-seater to be known as the Hengist. This would have been a troop carrier only, with the first models due in May 1941. There is some doubt whether any were actually made, since it was quickly seen that the Horsa was far better and production concentrated on that.

British gliders were made of wood, and the contracts went to furniture firms in order to save skilled labour. Unfortunately, the Mosquito and some other projected high-performance aircraft types were competing for the same materials and work force, and their priorities were higher so that glider production never entirely kept pace with demand.

The furniture firms proved well able to build gliders, which may say something for British furniture, but one other feature of the original concept proved hopelessly false. It was assumed, on no experience at all, that to fly a glider was something that could be done with the very minimum of training and the planners of 1940 saw the glider trains being flown by truck drivers who had been given a brief conversion course! It is almost incredible now to imagine the naivety of the officers who put forward this idea in all seriousness – when across the Channel the Germans were consulting their civilian gliding champions on every move. Typical of the thinking in the British Army was the specification for a flying jeep. The photograph shows the elements of the design clearly enough, and it is to the credit of the manufacturer that it flew at all, but it was intended that this remarkable machine should be piloted by its regular driver, who discarded the wings on landing and picked up his crew who had parachuted from the tug, and drove into battle! Only one was made, and it obviously flew at least once, but the dangers were too awful to contemplate. Even the Horsa was not originally meant to carry more than a motorcycle and sidecar, and it was sheer luck that the jeep fitted it.

The Horsa was intended to carry parachutists. With no suitable aircraft it seemed the best way. On the Mk 1 there were two doors, one on either side, and staggered. They could be opened in flight by sliding upwards inside the fuselage, and the tactical reason for this was that they could be used for machine-gun positions to defend the plane in flight. There was also an upper machine-gun aperture in the wing, and one in the tail. Needless to say, none was ever used. Continuing the parachuting theme were two short rails over the doors to which the individual jumper would have hooked his static line as he came forward to jump. His weapons and supplies would have been dropped in panniers through the doors, or in containers hung from the wings. Six strong points were built into the wing centre section to carry the containers, although it was necessary to jettison the undercarriage to drop from them, the glider subsequently landing on its central skid. It was quickly found, however, that landings were far better with the undercarriage left on.

The Horsa was mainly a plywood machine, and very little metal was used in its manufacture. The fuselage was a plywood tube, built around circular ribs, and the tail was a plywood cone tilted up to give a straight line along the top of the fuselage. The wings and tail were wood frames covered with ply and fabric, and the wing centre section was permanently fixed to the upper fuselage, but the outer wing panels were removable. The pilots sat in a 'glasshouse' in the extreme nose where they had a remarkably good view, but virtually no protection from a crash. Their situation was even worse if the load that they were carrying happened to break loose as they then became the jam in the sandwich, and on a few occasions this did occur. The pilots were in contact with the tug crew until the tow rope was dropped, but had no other link with either the ground or other aircraft. They were remarkably brave men who carried much responsibility on their shoulders during the flight, and they had to become part of the land battle when they had delivered their load. By the time of the Normandy landings the British glider pilots had become so valuable that special arrangements were made to extract them on D + 1 so that they could fly in a second lift.

The Mk 1 Horsa loaded its heavy equipment through a door in the port side just aft of the nose. It was intended to accept a motor cycle and sidecar only which, in 1940, was foreseen as being all that an airborne force needed in the way of transport. It was, therefore, sheer luck that a jeep and also the 6-pounder anti-tank gun could be fitted through the same door. Much manoeuvring and juggling was required, and something quicker was needed to get the loads out. The answer was to take off the conical tail section complete, and photos of wartime landing zones clearly show Horsas with their tails swung round and pulled away from the fuselage. Removing the tail was not always easy. The proper way was to unscrew the six bolts which held it on, but these sometimes jammed, and an emergency drill was used to blow it off with a ring of explosive cord. Of course, this ruined the glider, and finally a form of quick release was evolved. The Mk 2 Horsa appeared in 1943, too late for Sicily, and had several improvements on the Mk 1. The most noticeable was the loading door which was now in the nose. The whole nose section was hinged to allow both loading and unloading, using a ramp, which was much more straightforward. However, the nose was vulnerable to damage on landing, and the tail-removal technique was retained. Another minor change was that a single tow rope ran from a point under the nose to the tug instead of the original Y-shaped rope running to two attachment points under the wings.

The Hamilcar

The Horsa was the workhorse of the airborne forces, and carried most of the medium-weight equipment in an airborne assault. However, it could not carry armoured vehicles or combinations of vehicles, and early in 1941 a design was laid down for what became the Hamilcar. General Aircraft undertook to build it, and its loaded weight was just ten times that of the Hotspur, their only other design. The actual weights were 3,600lb to 36,000lb. A half-scale model was flown first of all but even so, the prototype was flying within twelve months of the design being agreed. It was the largest wooden aircraft constructed in the UK during the war, and it was much more an aeroplane without motors than the popular idea of a glider. The wing loading was 21·7lb/sq ft, which meant that it flew quite fast and needed enormous flaps worked by compressed air to land safely. It was an efficient load carrier as it could lift its own weight, and the payload was 17,500lb. This enabled it to carry such items as the Tetrach tank, the Locust tank, or the D.4 small bulldozer or a host of other equipments including the 25-pounder gun. All loads were put in through the nose

An M-22 Locust tank driving out of a Hamilcar glider. (*Author*)

which swung to the right. Unloading was by the same route, and there was no provision for alternative unloading through the tail or anywhere else. The arrangements for opening the nose became most ingenious, if not actually alarming. The vehicle would start up its engine while still in flight, and a small pipe led the exhaust to the sides. On landing the driver pulled a lanyard which disconnected the lashings, and drove forward. A mechanical trip released the nose which swung to the right out of the way, and the tank or carrier went straight out of the fuselage bumping over the low sill onto the ground. The usual time for this exciting manoeuvre was 15sec from start to finish. But, in fact, the tank loads were at the limit of the Hamilcar's capacity, and at least one glider disintegrated in the air on the way to the Rhine crossing when it was caught in the slipstream of several tugs flying ahead of it.

The Hamilcar was so big that it needed the largest and most powerful aeroplanes to pull it. Four-engined bombers were used, and the Halifax the most often. The tug crews had a difficult task, flying for most of the time at little more than their stalling speed and when the landing zone approached having to come down to a suicidally low height without being able to

This shows the degree of organisation needed for a successful glider operation. Horsas and Hamilcars lined up along the runway with their Halifax tugs in echelon on each side. Early 1944. (*Imperial War Museum*)

take evasive action. Many were lost in this way, and it was always a strain for the RAF to find enough tugs for the Hamilcars. In an effort to reduce this demand for tugs and also to improve the take-off performance and operational range of the towed glider in the tropics, the Mk 10 Hamilcar Air Freighter was built. It was a Hamilcar with two engines, and apart from these the only major differences were in the cockpit which became a 'blister' on top of the fuselage, and a stronger undercarriage. When the Japanese surrendered, the first machines were undergoing flight trials in England and proving successful. Under tow they carried the same load as the glider; under power with full fuel tanks it was reduced to 3,000lb. Their development was immediately dropped, and the idea was taken no further.

Other gliders

Another glider idea which never became more than a prototype was an Australian venture called the DH G2. In 1942, alarmed by the very real possibility of an invasion, the Australian Government found that it had scarcely any strategic trans-

September 1944. Loading a medical jeep of the 101st Airborne Division into a Waco CG-4 Hadrian. This glider has the Griswold nose towing point and, unusually, radio aerials. During loading the tail is supported by struts. (*US Army*)

port for its small defence forces. It was most necessary that they should be capable of being moved rapidly from one part of the country to another, and there were no transport aircraft. A glider was quickly designed by De Havilland of Australia which could be towed by the few elderly aircraft that were available. It was predominantely wooden in construction, high winged and resembled the later Waco Hadrian. Three were made before shipments of Hadrians arrived from the USA and the danger was averted.

USA

The other glider which was used in quantity in World War II was the American Waco CG-4A, made by the Waco Aircraft Corporation. This was the standard glider of the US airborne forces, and was also used on occasions by British air-landing troops. When in British use it was known as the Hadrian, but to the US Army it was never anything more romantic than CG-4. It was smaller than the Horsa, particularly in the length of the fuselage, and carried fifteen troops or 3,800lb. Like all the World War II cargo gliders, it was a high-wing design, and

CG-13 gliders in Europe, May 1945. This was a larger and more robust version of the CG-4, but not many were made and few saw active service. (*US Army*)

the fuselage was almost square in section. Unusually, it was made of steel tube, fabric-covered. This gave it a great advantage in storage, the more so in the tropics, and it was used by General Wingate's Chindits for their incursions into Burma in 1944, as well as by 1st Airborne Division in North Africa in 1943. Fifteen was an awkward number of men to carry because it did not fit the size of the infantry units, and, more significantly, it was fewer than the C-47 Dakota would carry. It was, therefore, more economical in aircraft to fly parachutists than to tow a glider, and so it is that the American air assaults were far more parachute operations than were the British, with whom the ratio of glider-borne to parachuted units was frequently one to three and sometimes one to two.

But despite its smaller size the Waco was heavily used, and in one respect its lower weight was a positive advantage, for it was easier to tow and the tug used less fuel. In August 1944 the glider force for the invasion of Southern France was held up in its flight from Italy by mist, and had to circle over Corsica while the visibility cleared on the landing zones. The Waco tugs had enough fuel to do this, but the Horsa tugs had to turn back to their base and take on more before once more setting out. Fortunately, there was no tactical penalty for this delay, but it could have been serious in a different setting.

The load-carrying limitations of the CG-4 led to the Waco Corporation to develop the CG-13, which was a larger version but it arrived too late for the European operations, although some were sent over. A small number of CG-13s was used in the Luzon operation in the Philippines, where they were entirely successful but after that brief debut they were not used again. Still pursuing the same theme, CG-8 was brought out after the war, and only a few prototypes were ever built. This glider resembled a motorless version of the Fairchild C-119. It was all metal, covered in a metal skin, and far too expensive for the concept. It was also too late, for already short-take-off-and-landing aircraft were on the drawing board, as well as practical means of heavy dropping.

The Waco was loaded from the nose, like the Horsa 2 (which may have been inspired by the Waco) but the nose swung up and out of the way. Two small ramps let down, and the tail could be supported on a jack so that the floor was steady during loading. One jeep or one gun could be lifted, and the unloading sequence was not far different from the Hamilcar, though in the case of the Waco the nose was actually lifted by a rope attached to the back bumper of the jeep. As the jeep ran forward the rope pulled the nose up, where two stays locked it. The jeep slipped its rope and went, and in later models the rope was released automatically so that there was hardly any need to even stop on the way out. It didn't always work like that. Maurice Tugwell relates how in Burma one Waco came in with a small bulldozer on board. It came in at speed, raced across the landing zone, crashed into some trees, threw off its wings, and stopped. The dozer, however, went on. The pilots were flung up into the air as it tore out below them, smashing everything in its path, including the cockpit stays. As they slammed back into place the pilot is reputed to have said to his partner 'That's just the way I planned it!'

The Chindit operations in Burma also saw an experiment in

gliding which was not often tried elsewhere. This was the double tow. For the first landing on to the 'Broadway' landing zone each C-47 towed two Wacos, the gliders being held out to each side by their pilots. It was not a great success; some tow ropes parted and in every case the tugs found that they had taken on more than they bargained for with the extra weight of the second glider, for in training the loads had been comparatively light, but when actually going into action every machine was overloaded to the absolute limit of safety. Later in the war the double-tow method was perfected. On the Rhine crossing in 1945 many of the glider trains were using double tow for the Wacos. It was a method which required more skill from the glider pilot than the single tow, and of course it could not be used in bad weather or darkness without considerable risk.

Another experiment was the snatch technique for retrieving gliders from small landing zones where a tug could not land. It worked in the following way. The glider was placed at the extreme downwind end of the cleared area, and its tow rope led forward to a loop which was held up on two poles, so that there was a straight rope between them, and the slack lying on the ground. The tug was always a C-47 Dakota which flew in low and as slowly as it dared trailing a hook. The instant that this hook connected with the line between the poles the pilot opened the throttles and climbed away. The hook from the plane was attached to another line in the fuselage of the tug and this was wound round a friction brake. The tow rope was the usual nylon which stretched appreciably under load. There was, therefore, little actual jerk as the line tightened, and to a spectator the glider seemed to be a long time making up its mind to move, for the tow rope pulled out a long way before overcoming the inertia of the Waco. Suddenly it would go, accelerating more swiftly than for the normal air tow, and becoming airborne in a surprisingly short run. From then on the flight was fairly normal. In the Chindit operations at least one small bulldozer was moved from one landing area to another by this method, and on another occasion the crew of a crashed plane was rescued from a remote mountain valley where there was neither room to make an airstrip nor was it feasible to walk out. It was also regularly used in the 1944–5 campaign in

September 1943. An early example of twin tow. A C-47 and two CG-4 gliders. (*US Army*)

northern Europe to evacuate casualties from the forward areas.

By the end of the war trials were being made in snatching single men by the same method, but it was never used on operations, and it is now difficult to discover if a live man was ever snatched at all. Certainly dummies were snatched, and this was done most successfully at a display in 1948 to the great wonderment of the spectators, few of whom fancied themselves in the role of snatchee. The dummy sat in a special harness facing the plane as it approached. The plane then passed over his head and hooked up the line. Again the throttles were opened, the line stretched, and the man was whisked up into the sky at an angle of at least 30° and perhaps more. He was then winched into the plane, presumably with some special sort of winch to prevent his being battered along the fuselage side as he came in. As a spectacle the man-snatch has few equals, but as a serious method of moving one man in wartime it is rather a futile exercise, the whole purpose of which has now been replaced by the helicopter.

The same military display must have been almost the last

time that the full variety of military gliders and similar devices were on show, so quickly did they disappear after 1945. For the Normandy landings the Allies had over 2,500 gliders ready; there was a similar number for the Nijmegen and Arnhem operations, and nearly 1,400 for the Rhine crossing in March 1945. But these were the high-water mark of the glider for it was too expensive to keep in service in peace. About 10 per cent were recovered from each operation and used again, the remainder being completely lost. They were either shot down on the approach to the landing zone or, more usually, damaged beyond repair by the landing itself, the removing of the load, or enemy action on the ground. Maintenance was high on fabric-covered structures, and training flights damaged many machines urgently needed for operations, so that there was a steady loss rate without going to war at all. But there was another price to be added to the cost of gliders, a price in terms of skilled men. Every glider which flew to battle required the services of four pilots, two in the tug and two in the glider. The two in the glider would not come back, the tug pilots might. If both were shot down it would be an expensive flight, and too often that expense was demanded. Both tugs and gliders were shot down in large numbers at Arnhem and Nijmegen, and on the Rhine crossing the British lost 27 per cent of their glider pilots on the approach flight. The US lost fewer that day, but almost made up for it in tug casualties caused by using a lower release height. The loss of a tug was a serious matter, for there were never enough aircraft at any time. Whilst the C-47 Dakota was an excellent tug, it was also equally excellent at many other tasks, and the decisions as to which use to put it to must at times have been very difficult to make. The same can be said on the German side, where the Junkers 52 was the maid of all work and just as much in demand as the Dakota. The RAF dragged in all possible machines to tow gliders, as is related elsewhere, and considerable persuasion was needed to get them to release bombers for towing the Hamilcars.

Russia

Both Japan and the Soviet Union made some limited use of

gliders, and several other countries showed an interest in their possibilities. Few carried their researches much beyond a limited run of prototypes, but the Soviet Union followed the lead of Germany and Britain, and in 1941 began series production of the Antonov A-7.

The Antonov A-7

The A-7 was markedly similar in outline, shape, size and payload to the German DFS 230, indeed so closely do they resemble each other that at first glance it is easy to assume that the A-7 is merely a captured DFS with a red star painted on it. In fact, the differences ran a little deeper. The construction was entirely of wood with a fabric covering. There was a single pilot and the payload was nine fully equipped troops or their equivalent weight in cargo. The undercarriage was a single two-wheeled axle below the fuselage and a tail-skid.

Four hundred of these gliders were built and were chiefly used in reinforcing and resupplying the many partisan groups operating behind the German lines. The towing aircraft were apparently many and varied, with the IL-2 being the most frequently used. How often these operational A-7s were recovered and re-used is not known, and it seems that the fleet of 400 was rapidly used up. Other designs were tried and at least five were pursued more or less seriously, though none got beyond the prototype stage. The most promising one was the Polikarpov BDP S-1, a striking design with a noticeably smooth outline. Started in 1941, this was to be a twenty-seater with the alternative cargo capacity for a jeep and light field gun or similar equipment. The specification was very like that for the Horsa, and the construction was to have been of wood throughout. In the event the idea was dropped after the first model had completed its test flights, and in the winter of 1944 it was fitted with two 140hp engines in an effort to raise interest in powered gliders. However, this too failed.

The Tsybin TS-25

Soviet airborne forces had to wait until the war ended before they received any useful numbers of home-built gliders, and the first appeared in 1947. This was the Tsybin TS-25, built to meet a specification for a glider capable of carrying a payload of 4,500lb or twenty-five fully equipped troops. The crew of two sat side-by-side in a cabin above the fuselage and just forward of the wing leading edge. The square fuselage was covered in plywood, rounded at the corners, and faired into a rounded nose section. This nose section hinged to one side for loading and a simple tricycle undercarriage gave a very low loading step up to the main floor line.

The shoulder wing was braced by a single strut and was partly fabric covered. The wing area was 481sq ft which gave a wing loading of 13·7lb per sq ft at full load. The span was 53ft. Maximum gliding speed was 144mph, which could be reduced to 60mph for landing.

The TS-25 was unusual in that it was also intended for civil use and some experimental commercial services were actually tried, with apparently little success since they were soon dropped. Several hundred were accepted into military service by the aviation for the airborne troops.

The next year, 1948, two heavy transport gliders were evaluated. They were built to a specification which called for a $3\frac{1}{2}$ ton payload and nose-loading. The hold had to accept both wheeled and tracked vehicles, or provide seating for thirty-five troops. The crew was to be two. There were two contenders, from Ilyushin and Yakovlev.

The Ilyushin Il-32

This was a fairly conventional slab-sided design of box-like appearance. It was unusual in that it was built of metal throughout and unique in that both nose and tail sections were hinged and could be swung to the side to give clear access to the hold from either end. The two pilots sat in a small 'glass-house' in the nose section and moved with it when it opened. Despite its merits, the Il-32 was not chosen and the decision went to Yakovlev.

The Yakovlev YAK-14

A very conventional design of distinctly angular outline, this glider had wings set well back along the fuselage, and the pilots sat in tandem in a small 'glass-house' which was blistered on to the port side of the fuselage top. This offset gave the machine a most curious and lop-sided appearance when it was viewed from anywhere in the front arc. The pilots, incidentally, had to climb up outside the fuselage using external hand-holds and steps. The nose section swung upwards for access to the hold and the floor was very close to the ground. The YAK-14 was successful, and 413 were built altogether. The construction was of wood and fabric and it was probably the cheapness of these materials which helped it to be chosen instead of the Il-32. When fully loaded it weighed almost 15,000lb, and it must have been beyond the abilities of an Il-2 to pull it. There is some doubt still as to what tug was actually used, but the most likely are any of the elderly medium bombers which were plentiful at that time in the Soviet Air Force.

The YAK-14 was the last Soviet military glider, and also the last military glider of any nation to be built in useful quantity. The YAK continued flying for several years, no doubt decreasing in quantity with each passing season, and finally disappeared in the mid-1950s when the first experiments were made with heavy dropping. By that time the Soviet airborne divisions had withdrawn into central Russia where they were kept out of sight from Western attachés and journalists, and their development could be pursued in almost total secrecy.

Japan

Japan, like so many other countries, produced a positive rash of glider designs, nearly all of which were still-born. The main reason for the failure of the Japanese gliders is that they all arrived too late. Almost all were built to specifications issued in 1941, yet only two flew before 1944, and by that time Japan was no longer seriously thinking in terms of airborne assaults. In general the specifications show more originality and enterprise than did the Soviet ones of the same period, and one can only be surprised at the apparent lethargy of the manufacturers who took them up.

The first successful design was the Maeda Kul-1 which was originated by the army's first glider specification in 1940. This was a very small machine carrying only a pilot and six or seven men, and it was used only for training. It was unusual for such a small glider in being a twin-boom layout, and a second model in 1942 reverted to a single fuselage of a lifting aerofoil section. However, only small numbers of the first version were made and the second never got beyond the initial prototype.

The next model was the Kugisho MXY-5 built for the Navy. It carried only eleven troops and no more than a dozen were ever built. There followed, in fairly quick succession, the Kokusai KU-8, the Kokusai KU-7, the Fukuda KU-9, and the Nihon Kogota KU-11. All started their flight trials in 1944 and only the KU-8 was adopted. However, the KU-7 was the most interesting one as it was the only heavy transport glider to be built in Japan. Development started in 1942, and the layout is markedly similar to the Gotha 242, which machine may well have influenced the designer, but the KU-7 was much larger. Its loaded weight was 26,000lb against 16,000 pounds for the Go-242. The central nacelle was quite well streamlined and the four main wheels of the undercarriage were half-submerged into the underside. The intended load was to be a light tank or thirty-two troops, both being loaded through the upward-swinging rear-fuselage section. Flight trials of the prototype were quite successful but the war had turned in favour of the Allies and further development had to be dropped.

The KU-8, on the other hand, was uninteresting but successful. Its origin is a little involved, apparently stemming originally from a twin-engined high-wing light-transport plane, a most unusual beginning for any glider. The second version of the KU-8 was produced early in 1944, and deliveries continued until March 1945. The fuselage was of steel tube, fabric covered, and the nose hinged sideways for loading. Wings and tail were of wood. The crew of two sat in the hinging nose section, and the hold accommodated twenty troops or a jeep and a light gun. Unusually, there was only a two-wheeled undercarriage which must have complicated loading and unloading. The KU-8 actually took part in operations, the only Japanese glider ever so used, though even then it was only in a reinforcement role. A number of them was captured on Luzon during the liberation of the Philippines.

This completes the formal history of military load-carrying

gliders and, as for all new aircraft, oddities of design were tried in an effort to get the most from the Laws of Aerodynamics.

Design oddities

The first true oddity appeared in 1942 when the GAL Hotspur had been relegated to being a trainer. In an effort to produce a glider with a useful load, the manufacturer joined two fuselages together with a short constant-chord wing. The outer wing panels from the Mk II were retained, giving an overall span of 58ft and a new tailplane joined the rear fuselages. The pilot was in the port cockpit and the maximum load was intended to be fifteen troops, a useful number, but not, it will be remembered, a tactical sub-unit. The prototype was first flown in August 1942 being towed by a Whitley, but soon afterwards it crashed and was wrecked, and the idea was dropped.

There was always some interest in using the glider fuselage to assist lift. The easiest way was to build it in a rectangular section with the longer sides forming the horizontal members, in other words, wider than the depth. The side profile of the fuselage was then built to the shape of an aerofoil and it immediately became a very narrow and rather inefficient wing. The most advanced example of this theory was the DFS 331 of 1941 which was not developed but other designs carried the idea farther, albeit in a slightly different way. The idea behind the Junkers Ju-322 and the General Airborne XCG-16 was that the fuselage should become a total lifting surface with the tail supported on booms.

The Junkers design used a massive wing with a conventional-looking fuselage running back to the tail, but this fuselage disappeared completely into the wing and passengers, cargo and crew were all contained in the centre section. The span of the enormous wing was 203ft and the intended payload was 44,000lb; sufficient for a PZKW IV tank, an SP gun with its crew, or an 88mm AA gun and towing lorry. This ambitious intention never materialised because constructional difficulties reduced the available capacity to 26,000lb, which even so was remarkable, when the first prototype flew in March 1941. The undercarriage could not stand up to the loads imposed by take-off at full weight and a special trolley was used which fell away when the machine became airborne. As it happened, the Ju 322 or Mammoth, as it was to be called, showed itself to be almost unmanageable in the air and the idea was dropped in May 1941. The difficulty lay in the lack of effective side area, which caused the machine to yaw from side to side. The towing aircraft for the flight trials was a Junkers 90 four-engined transport, which only just managed to drag the Mammoth into the air despite a 3-mile overshoot path which had been cut into the forest beyond the runway end!

The Mammoth was a failure, and its huge size would probably have defeated the available airfields and tug aircraft had it actually come into service. The only other glider 'flying-wing', the XCG-16, failed also, but for a different reason. In this case it was too late for the US Army contract, which was taken from it by the WACO CG-13. The XCG-16 had a span of 91ft – less than half the Mammoth – and a payload of 10,000lb, or forty troops, or two 75mm airborne howitzers and their crews. This cargo was carried in the bulbous centre section, the front of which hinged upwards for loading. The tail was carried on two narrow booms and flight characteristics were quite pleasant. However, only one prototype was built and flown.

Another unsuccessful American oddity was an amphibious glider. The US Navy specified two types in 1942, but awarded contracts only for the smaller version. Two prototypes were test-flown in 1943 before the scheme was cancelled, and both were very nearly unique in being low-wing layouts. The only other low-wing glider was a Turkish model. The amphibians had ply-covered planing hulls and jettisonable tricycle undercarriages. In other respects they were normal for the time, with a payload of ten troops. So far as is known, these two were the only gliders ever made for intentional landings on water.

The last of what one might call the 'blind alleys' of military gliding was an experimental short-landing version of the DFS 230. The success of the Eben Emael operation had convinced the Germans of the value of gliders for *coup de main* assaults. The difficulty was that many of these depended upon the gliders landing in very restricted spaces, which could be hazardous. It has already been related how retro-rockets were used successfully to achieve short landing runs, but another idea actually tried on a DFS 230 was to remove the wings and fit a three-bladed autogiro rotor. This rotor free-wheeled and the glider could then be towed quite safely at 150mph carrying a load of 1 ton. On landing the run was less than 20yd, but stability in flight was poor and the idea had to be abandoned.

Gliders formed only a short chapter in the history of airborne warfare; almost every other type of equipment has survived in one form or another until the present day, but the glider disappeared soon after the war ended and now none remain. They were an expensive way to move military equipment. They were an expedient, an awkward one and an expensive one, but an expedient none the less and like all expedients they were dropped as soon as something better came along.

6 Ground Mobility

The paradox of airborne forces is that they get to their battle-field quicker than anyone else, and can travel immense distances in getting there, but having arrived they are scarcely more mobile than was Alexander the Great or Napoleon. In other words, an airborne force has great strategical mobility, but little tactical mobility. Throughout World War II, and to a great extent today, the speed of movement of the parachute force was limited to that of the marching man. From the very beginning it was realised that this was a serious limitation which would require to be overcome if it was not to affect operations.

Mobility requires vehicles; vehicles require aeroplanes to carry and deliver them, and throughout World War II it was hardly possible to carry vehicles except in gliders. In the early German airborne operations even gliders were absent and in at least one instance the ground operations suffered severely as a result. For without vehicles the parachute force can only capture and hold a limited objective until the ground forces push through to them and relieve them. Where this did not happen, such as Arnhem, the airborne force has either to fight until it is overcome, or surrender, or split up and try to escape in small parties. It cannot conduct a battle of manoeuvre against its opponents, nor can it easily subdue one objective and move away to take on another unless that second one is quite close.

Germany

The Germans did what they could to overcome this limitation by providing all the wheels that could be carried. The trouble was that not many could be. The Junkers 52 was too restrictive in space to allow anything more than a small container to be carried underneath it, and the door was too small to allow any sort of vehicle to be pushed out. The first requirement was to ease the burden of moving containers across the drop zone. A loaded container weighed several hundred pounds and it was

The Flying Jeep, a jeep fitted with a fuselage, tail and autogiro rotors for towing behind an aeroplane. Only one was built, and proved difficult to fly. (*ML Aviation Ltd*)

often highly undesirable to have to unpack it on the drop zone and carry off the contents in part. The obvious answer was to put wheels on it, and this enabled a container to be pulled for a few hundred yards by two or more men. The versions used in Crete had a folding handle and two wheels which could be quickly taken out, clipped into place, and the whole device dragged away.

This at least got the loads off the open spaces of the drop zone, but small wheels are useless for cross-country as others were to find out later on in the war, and once the container had been pulled in to some central collecting point the problem of how to move such items as mortar ammunition still remained. A container weighing perhaps 200lb and running on two wheels of, say, 18in diameter will go easily enough on a tarmac road (but note that it only goes at the speed of the man pulling it), but it becomes a devilish and exhausting contraption to move across farmland. In ploughed land it sinks and has to be half carried, half dragged; it has to be lifted over ditches, heaved over hedges, and carried bodily through streams. The towing team spend more time carrying it than they do pulling it. The answer is to move along tracks and paths, but this is not always where the infantry want to go, and it is usually where a defender first sites his weapons. So the wheeled container only solved part of the problem. For the Germans there was no other means of mobility until the air-transported force could land in its Junkers. It was then possible to bring in some motor-cycle and sidecar outfits, as well as a few half-track motor-cycles.

The German airborne used the standard Wermacht BMW motor-cycle and sidecar, with the well-known flat-twin engine of 750cc. With this they not only towed trailers, but also used it to drag a 3·7cm anti-tank gun while the four-man crew sat on the machine. Naturally, such overloading could only be done on a flat road surface since the motor-cycle could not possibly carry such a weight across country. The British thought of trying sidecar combinations when they were planning their airborne troops, but it never came to anything. The Germans also had a few larger motor-cycle combinations with half-tracked rear wheels. These were much larger and heavier vehicles and were used by normal infantry as ammunition carriers; a few were tried by the airborne troops but they could not be used for operations until the Gotha 242 appeared to carry them.

One other idea of the Germans, which did not prove successful, was to use ponies to pull guns. Some little mountain Haflingers were carried in Junkers 52s for the operations in Holland in 1940, but at Waalhaven airfield their natural fears got the better of them and they panicked. They were never tried again. Bizarre though the idea seems now, the German Army used horses throughout the war, and in 1940 it was probably the natural thing to do, even for an airborne army. The ponies were meant to lie down during the approach flight and to remain calm when under fire on the ground. It was more than they could manage.

Great Britain

The British realised from the earliest days of their airborne development that if a parachute force was going to operate in any way other than just as a raiding force it would need heavy weapons and the vehicles to move them. At first there was an aberration in the thinking as the German idea of motor-cycles

A posed photograph of a soldier unloading a folding Welbike from a CLE container. In the background is another man riding one. (*Imperial War Museum*)

was pursued, but this never came to anything. Its only effect was to direct the designers of the Horsa glider to install a light floor and a small door in their glider, but fortunately the floor could be easily strengthened when the jeep appeared and the door was just large enough. But the solo motor-cycle was used in quite large numbers. The standard military machine was 500cc and rather too heavy for air delivery, so a much smaller and lighter one of 125cc was adopted. Generally these were made by the James firm, or were Royal Enfields. It was powerful enough to carry a man at a reasonable speed over rough ground, big enough to clear potholes and obstacles, yet light enough to be picked up and carried when necessary. It could be dropped either as a door bundle from the C-47, or from the bomb bay of the Halifax. An attempt to use an even lighter and smaller version was less successful.

The Welbike

This was a tiny machine of 98cc which folded into a standard CLE container. It was known as the Welbike and was specially designed for airborne use. The handle-bars, steering head and saddle pillar folded down onto the machine and made a load 51in long, 15in wide, and weighing 70lb. As a military vehicle it was too light and too small. It lacked the power for cross-

145

country driving and so had to be driven on tracks and paths. The wheels were too small to negotiate potholes or similar obstacles, and with an average-sized man the entire outfit was perilously near to being overloaded. But it was remarkably ingenious in design and construction and although it may have offered little more improvement in mobility than was obtained with the wheeled container, it gave encouragement to its users that at least some designers were aware of their special problems and were tackling them. After the war a civilian version gained a certain amount of popularity for personal transport during the difficult days of fuel rationing in the late 1940s and early 1950s.

Bicycles

Another obvious and cheap way to improve the individual man's ability to move about the battlefield was to give him a bicycle. Bicycles have been tried for military purposes since they first were invented, but they have never been any better than a very partial success, and one might almost say a failure. There was no reason to suppose that they would be any better in the hands of airborne troops. Nor were they. Cycles have to move on prepared surfaces, and although they are quick and quiet they only carry one man and very little additional weight. They are easily damaged, not least by parachuting though that is explained elsewhere, and once damaged are virtually useless. They might have had a limited value in the Arnhem operation where there were roads enough, but even then it is difficult to imagine their being used for much more than message carrying. The idea of a company of infantry pedalling down a road in enemy territory simply doesn't make military sense. Nevertheless the airborne were forced to accept bicycles, lightweight, folding – for the most part they used them in and around barracks for routine duties.

Wheels

However, at the same time as the motor-cycles were being produced, the British were also following the German idea of wheels for containers though in this case the wheels were not actually attached to the container but were in the form of a

A jeep towing the US version of the British 6-pounder anti-tank gun off the landing zone. Rhine crossing, May 1945. (*Imperial War Museum*)

barrow which folded up into a container and was used to carry the contents off the drop zone. A slight variation on the German original, and perhaps more time-consuming, but on the credit side it was more flexible in the loads that it could carry and it was lighter and less bulky. Naturally it suffered from the same defects as the wheeled container when it came to cross-country work. On roads, however, the barrow did sterling work and was still in use at the time of the Rhine crossing in 1945. Motive power not only came from men pushing, but from teams in front with drag ropes.

The Jeep

The saviour for the battlefield mobility of the Allied airborne forces was the arrival of that remarkable vehicle – the jeep. It came just in time for the British and enabled them to make the necessary adjustments to the design of the Horsa glider before any had been turned out in mass production. For the Americans it was early enough to enable the CG-4 to be designed around it, and for all the Allies it was the vehicle which would tow the artillery pieces, and carry all the other weapons and their ammunition, as well as the heavy radio sets, batteries and charging engines. If the C-47 flew the Allied airborne armies, it was the jeep which moved them once they were on the ground.

But lest one should imagine that the arrival of the jeep implied instant mobility for all, this would be wrong. The soldier in the rifle company was still walking, and the overall speed of the battalion was no faster. What the jeep did was to make it possible for that battalion to take its support weapons with it, and to carry many other pieces of equipment, not least of which were stretchers and medical supplies. In time the doctors found that they could pack enough surgical equipment into a jeep trailer to set up a tiny operating theatre in the field. The wounded could not only be properly treated, but they could be moved also. The trailer which went behind the jeep carried a nominal half ton. It invariably ended up with nearly twice as much, but some care had to be taken in the loading when it was being carried in a glider, otherwise the centre of gravity of the glider was affected, not to mention the effect on the flying characteristics as well. Many jeeps towed two trailers and all trailers had a towing eye on the front and back, so that these 'trains' could be made up.

One other type of trailer used by the British was very similar to the standard jeep type, but it was slightly smaller and much lighter in construction and intended to be expendable. Thin sheet metal was used for the sides and floor, reinforced with wood. The wheels were motor-cycle type, on a simple axle with no springs. These trailers were intended to be filled with ammunition and loaded into gliders to make up the maximum flying weight, should the actual load of the glider not go to the limit. The trailer was pulled off the landing zone by the glider pilots, and dumped at the rendezvous point, or they might hitch it on to a passing jeep going to the same place. It had both handles and a tow hook. When it got to the RV it was left, as a wheeled stack of ammunition, ready to be taken wherever it was needed, and when the ammunition had been used the trailer was dumped. Many went to Arnhem, and all stayed there. A very few survived the war, and only one now remains intact in the Airborne Forces Museum.

Armour

The jeep provided the means of moving most of the weapons of

148

An overloaded British jeep leaving the dropping zone. Rhine crossing, May 1945. (*Imperial War Museum*)

the airborne force, but there was always the nagging feeling that armoured vehicles were needed to give the essential protection from enemy armoured attacks and to drive into defended areas where the lightly armed infantry could not penetrate. Luckily there had been a suitable tank in Britain since 1938, known as the A 17 and subsequently the Light Mk VII. Production was slow, partly because of War Office policy to concentrate on cruiser and heavy tanks, and partly from a change of contractor and bomb damage to the plant. The first production model came off the line in November 1940 and finally 177 were made. Production stopped with another change in policy which allocated armoured cars for reconnaissance work, and the Mk VII found itself without a real job to do. The name was changed to Tetrach in 1943 and it was adopted as a glider-borne tank. 6th Airborne Division formed an airborne reconnaissance regiment which was to be equipped with the tank, and the Hamilcars were tested in carrying them. Only one squadron of the regiment received Tetrachs and they took them to Normandy on D-Day. The contribution made by the Tetrach in that operation was

Polish paratroopers demonstrating the airborne trolley which they have just unpacked from a container. (*Imperial War Museum*)

limited, and although a few were also taken on the Rhine crossing, the battle history of the tank is modest. It seems likely that had more been employed they could have made a greater impact; there is no doubt that there was a crying need for them, as indeed there still is an urgent need for a powerful airborne armoured vehicle.

The Tetrach was a very light tank indeed, weighing 16,800lb fully loaded and equipped. The crew was two men, a driver and a commander who was also the gunner for the 2-pounder main gun. The commander must have had his hands full in action for not only was he directing the driver, but he was also selecting targets, traversing the turret, loading and firing the 2-pounder, and firing the Besa machine-gun when needed. Protective armour was thin, only 14mm – fractionally over half an inch – at the thickest point and 4mm over much of the vehicle. A peculiarity of the Tetrach which makes it easily recognizable was its four large road wheels on each side. These were independently sprung and steerable so that minor changes of direction were achieved by bending the flexible track. It was a fast little vehicle – 40mph could be reached on roads and 28mph cross-country, though that second figure was naturally subject to variations according to the terrain. A few survived the war and remained on strength until the gliders disappeared in 1949.

The only other tank to be used in airborne operations was the American M22, later named the Locust. This was the first tank to be actually designed as an airborne vehicle and the specification was finalised as early as May 1941. The requirement was for a tank weighing not more than 8 tons and sufficiently small to be carried either under or inside a transport aeroplane. The pilot model was made by the autumn of 1941, a remarkably fast piece of work, and first production models appeared in the spring of 1943. Over 800 were made before production stopped in February 1944, but it was never used in action by the US Army and the main reason was that they lacked either a glider or an aeroplane to carry it. At least one Locust was slung beneath a C-54 for air transport, but it could not be parachuted, because to get it beneath the fuselage the turret had to be removed and carried inside the plane. A large number of Locusts was given to the British Army and some were carried in Hamilcars. A few were used on the Rhine crossing operation, but that was their only combat use. It seems a sad ending for a tank that started with much promise.

The Locust was almost exactly the same size as the Tetrach, differing only in inches, although slightly smaller in every dimension. The weight was the same, and the gun – a 37mm M6 – very nearly the same as the 2-pounder. But the armour was thicker, 25mm at the thickest points and 9mm elsewhere, and the crew was three men, which would have made its tactical handling far easier. On paper the Locust looks to have been a better design all round than the Tetrach, which might be expected in view of the rapid improvement in tank design which came about once the war started. It is a pity that the effort which went into both tanks was never really utilised to the full.

7 Uniforms and Personal Equipment

Germany

From the very beginning the uniform of the German airborne troops was different from that of the army. Being Luftwaffe, they wore the standard Luftwaffe uniform with yellow collar rank patches and the regimental title embroidered on the lower sleeve. Officers had the title in aluminium-wire thread, other ranks used silver-coloured linen thread. This jacket was the parade uniform and was not worn when jumping. For parachuting, and for operations, the recognised uniform was a loose-fitting gaberdine overall which was quite unlike any other German military dress. It was a long-sleeved baggy garment, closed by a zip all down the front. It had two short trouser legs which reached to about mid-thigh and the wearer had to step into it in the same way as any other pair of overalls. It was not particularly elegant, nor was it the most practical garment for a fighting soldier. The sleeves closed at the wrist with buttons or snap fasteners. There were two large side pockets and two chest pockets. These could carry a good proportion of the smaller items of personal kit needed by the soldier.

Originally this overall was olive green in colour, but this was replaced by a camouflage pattern of green and brown printed shapes in late 1941. This later pattern of overall had no legs to it; instead the front and back hems could be joined by snap fasteners between the legs to make a simple *culotte* and prevent the garment from riding up. This was far more practical, and the principle was copied by the British Denison smock. Badges of rank were worn on the sleeves and an embroidered Luftwaffe badge was sewn to the right breast. The parachutist badge was only worn on the parade jacket. There was a low turned-down collar, but no lapel straps or other embellishments. The pockets had flaps, but these were not held shut. For parachuting the jumper wore his personal equipment underneath his overall and on landing he removed the overall, took

A propaganda photo of German parachutists in Holland, May 1940. (*Imperial War Museum*)

off the equipment, replaced the overall, and finally put his equipment on again over the overall. He was now ready for battle. It must have taken several precious minutes, but the Germans held to a strong belief that it was necessary to have a smooth uncluttered outline when jumping.

The helmet was a modified standard pattern with a much smaller rim. There was therefore none of the usual swept-down portion at the back of the neck which distinguishes the German helmet, and the general shape of the parachuting helmet is nearer to a pudding basin than anything else. It was held on by a chinstrap which ran from three attachment points on the rim, one each side and one at the back. The Luftwaffe eagle was printed on the left side, facing forwards. In action the helmet was usually covered with a camouflaged cloth cover, and the early models had a rubber shock-absorbing strip around the rim.

Trousers were long and loose, in the style of the times, normally grey in colour and with expanding buttoned pockets on each side. They were tucked in to the tops of the boots. The boots were themselves different from the usual army pattern and were a high-laced design. Up to the Crete operation these boots laced at the sides, but after July 1941 the lacing was in front. The soles of both patterns were in thick rubber with a distinctive chevron ribbing grip.

153

On his hands the parachutist wore an elaborate pair of leather gauntlets, elasticated at the wrist. On his knees were probably rubber protectors to absorb the shock of the forward-roll landing, and he might also have elasticated athletes' bandage around each ankle. Alternatively he might have bandages around the knee and no rubber pads.

The personal equipment was the same leather pattern as was worn by infantry of the line and the only special item was a webbing bandolier which held 120 rounds of ammunition in twelve compartments. It was carried slung around the neck, with six compartments on either side, and the ends were tied to the belt. Although such a method means that the ammunition is always at hand when needed, it is a fatiguing way to carry a load. Later, when the *Fallschirmjaeger* were issued with the FG 42, the bandolier was reduced to eight compartments.

When the Germans first used their airborne army in the invasion of the Low Countries in 1940 there were stories of them dropping in disguises of all kinds, ranging from nuns to bakers' boys. Later, in Crete it was alleged that British uniforms had been worn, and in the Ardennes offensive of December 1944, the parachutists were said to be wearing American uniform. None of these stories is true, although they have gained much credence from the fact that wartime Allied propaganda saw no reason to decry them. In fact the *Fallschirmjaeger* always parachuted into operations wearing their uniform as described in this chapter. The disguised soldiers in Holland and Belgium in 1940 were a special intelligence unit who drove in civilian cars. In Crete only a fool would have worn British uniform as he would have been shot by his own side. In the Ardennes precisely thirty-six men infiltrated the American lines wearing GI clothing; none came from the airborne force. All were rounded up within two days, though their effect lasted much longer and did much harm to the Allied cause.

Great Britain

The British started by following the general lead of the Germans. A good deal of effort was put into designing special uniforms, special helmets, special shirts, in fact special everything

– until the War Office put a firm stop to it. One of these special ideas was to line ordinary battledress trousers with chamois leather, even down to the pockets. They were quite naturally useless and immediately discarded, as were the several patterns of shock-absorbing boots which were ideal for parachute landings but quite hopeless for any sort of walking.

Until a proper parachute-landing fall was evolved in 1941 the British used a modification of the German idea of a forward roll on hitting the ground. This required some protection for the man and rubber knee pads were copied from the Germans together with, on occasions, elbow pads. It was quite obvious that a special steel helmet would be needed as the then current 'soup plate' variety inherited from World War I was totally unsuitable for parachuting, if not downright dangerous. The first jumpers had no head guard at all, but the number of minor concussion cases and banged heads made it imperative that some protection be provided quickly. Until a suitable steel helmet could be made a rubber training helmet was hurriedly produced. It was a cloth helmet with a thick strip of sponge rubber wound around the sides in the form of a short cylinder. There was no protection at all on the top of the head, which just had cloth over it, and a cloth strap fastened under the chin.

This curious headgear became instantly popular. It gave excellent protection from the normal landing bump which the head often suffers, it was light, the fastening flap kept the ears warm in winter (quite a consideration when one is the instructor in a balloon cage) and yet the wearer could hear perfectly. The Air Force instructors continued to use the helmet until long after the war and a very few were still being jumped by 'old hands' in the 1960s, long after manufacture had ceased. It was issued to all troops for training until the policy changed in about 1943, when the steel helmet was used exclusively by troops under training. This helmet was specially designed for airborne forces, it had a smooth outline with no brim to catch in rigging lines or straps, and a three-point suspension for the chin strap which led to a leather cup under the chin itself. It was comfortable to wear but a little heavy, a price paid for protection from splinters—all helmet design is a compromise.

Fitting parachutes at Ringway, 1941/2. The corporal in the centre is wearing the experimental side-lacing boots and all are hanging respirators onto their harness. (*Keystone*)

A special jump jacket closely copied from the German one was also issued in 1940 and 1941. This was a simple long-sleeved jacket which came down nearly to the knees and was snap fastened down the front and between the legs. The intention was to give a smooth outline to the body and allow the wearing of web equipment without the danger of the harness catching in it. This particular jacket was superseded by an equally long one without sleeves, but the earlier one continued to be used, particularly in the Middle East and Palestine until nearly the end of the war. Men under training at Kabrit in the Suez Canal Zone in December 1942 were wearing the long-sleeved jump jacket, the rubber helmet, and most unusually – rubber knee pads. By this time knee pads were definitely out of fashion in Britain.

Wearing web equipment under a parachute harness was by no means easy. Any items which hung from the belt had to be turned up so that they were above the waist; if they were not the jumper rolled over them as he landed and the result was a bad bruise. If the parachutist was not carrying a kitbag he had to dispose of his small pack and this was done by hanging it around the neck by one of its carrying straps. It then hung on the chest and over this ungainly figure went the jump jacket. By now of course the man looked enormous, with a waist-line three times its normal size and numerous bumps and lumps around his middle. On top of this went the X-type parachute, its harness lengthened until it was in some cases near the limit of its adjustment. With the harness properly tightened down it was downright uncomfortable, particularly on a hot day. The enormous bulge in front made it quite difficult to see the ground as it came up, and utterly impossible to see one's feet. Landings were invariably heavy with none of the lithe athletic twists so beloved of the RAF instructors, and bruises were frequent. The British continued with this method of carrying personal equipment until the reserve parachute was introduced in 1956, and then adapted the American way of carrying all personal gear in a small bundle slung under the reserve. This bundle is then dropped in the same way as a kitbag, and this is what is done today. It is far easier for the soldier, and it takes very little more time on the drop zone to sort it all out.

The best known article of special clothing to be given to parachutists in the British Army was the Denison smock, a loose camouflaged jacket with plenty of pockets, long sleeves and a 'tail' which snap-fastened between the legs. It was invented by a Captain Denison as a general-purpose garment which would fit over the battle dress and give some weather protection in the cold and wet climate of Europe, yet at the same time allow free movement and provide space for carrying ammunition, food and personal items.

The Denison smock is still worn by the British airborne forces, indeed there has been little outward change in the clothing of the soldier since the end of the war, the main advances being in the use of man-made fibres, and the general designs are much the same as they were in 1945.

The USA

The US Army equipped its experimental platoon with flying suits when they were first formed. These suits were the usual one-piece overalls in dark-olive twill, buttoning at the wrist and ankle. In 1941 a change was made to a shiny and stronger

Arnhem 1944: British parachute troops in action. (*Imperial War Museum*)

material, but shortly after that it was found that such suits were quite unnecessary for the military parachutist and they were discarded. There is some reason to suppose that cost and manufacturing effort may have helped this decision for the airborne was expanding at a rapid rate, so also was the rest of the US Army, and there were far more urgent orders to be filled than jump suits. The experimental platoon also wore a cloth helmet very similar in shape to a flying helmet. Some of these helmets look as though they have strips of padding running along the top of the head rather in the manner of a cyclist's crash hat. It may be that there was little attempt at standardisation in the short time in which this form of head gear was in use, for by the spring of 1942 the US airborne had decided that parachutists could manage perfectly well with standard army clothing and equipment.

The US helmet of World War II was a very practical shape and it was just as good for airborne troops as it was for ground troops. There was no brim, or barely any brim, to catch in static lines or straps and it had a chin cup to hold it on the head. It was strong and comfortable and it is still in use today with virtually no alteration from its original design. The fatigue uniform that the parachutist wore was equally practical. A loose two-piece set of overalls in olive-drab twill with a multitude of pockets was standard for all ranks and like the helmet is little changed today.

Like the British, the American paratrooper wore his webbing equipment when parachuting, but unlike the British no outer jacket was put over it. In fact the fully equipped US paratrooper of World War II resembles a Christmas tree for all his equipment is hung around him and all plainly in view. The photograph of a parachutist climbing into a plane on page 56 gives a graphic idea of what it was like to carry a full load of combat gear as well as a parachute. With that load hung around one it is a blessed relief to get out of the door and let the parachute take the weight for a short while, even though it is usually followed by a rather heavy landing.

Japan

The first Japanese Army parachute troops to be encountered in action were wearing clothing not far different from that of aircrews, even down to the goggles. By early 1942 the parachute force which dropped into the Dutch East Indies wore dark green or khaki overalls. These overalls buttoned up to a high neckline, without a collar. There were no distinguishing marks or badges on this garment and it was discarded on landing. Underneath it the soldiers wore the normal tropical uniform of the Japanese army, again without any special airborne insignia. The helmet was a cloth-covered crash helmet of sorbo rubber. It fitted closely to the head and ears, buttoning under the chin in very much the same style as a flying helmet. It was also dropped on landing and a normal fatigue cap worn in place of it. The intention of this helmet was obviously for protection to the head in landing only.

Another type of uniform appeared in late 1942 and was apparently based on the German overall. In the Japanese version the length looks to have been rather less than in the German one and the cuffs do not button. Otherwise it was very similar in all aspects. It had rank patches on the collar, and four pockets. It was worn over the personal equipment and was changed round on landing as with the German type. This pattern was only issued in small numbers, though it may have been used more extensively in the training establishments. By 1944 the parachutists encountered on Leyte were wearing clothing and equipment that was indistinguishable from normal infantry.

The army parachute troops had special lightweight personal equipment consisting of a belt and shoulder straps in light webbing. On the belt were two rows of ammunition pouches, and carriers for the water-bottle, haversack, pistol etc. There are no records of back-packs being carried, although the men in the Leyte operation did carry bags of special equipment on their backs, or slung over their shoulders. However, there are indications that Leyte provided an exception to several rules, for each man also carried two small bags or pockets hanging from his belt and strapped to leg, in which he had demolition gear and explosive.

Originally the Japanese planned that each parachutist should carry three days' rations, but this was reduced to two days in early 1944. At the same time an iron ration was introduced which was a 7oz pack of rice wafers with an extract of mussel flesh, dried plums, preserved ginger, crushed bean meal and *mori* (a special compound made from seaweed). Parachutists dropped in Hunan province in the summer of 1944 carried a small box containing about 1¼lb of a white 'flour'. When mixed with water this became a nourishing paste which would keep a man going for several days.

Japanese trainees preparing to jump, 1968. Their equipment and uniform is entirely American, so is the plane. (*Keystone*)

A peculiarity of the Japanese airborne forces was that the navy had a separate organisation running in tandem with the army, but trained and equipped differently. The naval parachutists' uniform was a two-piece outfit of green material of a silk and cotton mixture. The trousers tapered and fitted underneath the instep and had five pockets. The jacket was hip length and snug fitting with elastic at the neck, waist and cuffs. This jacket had at least five pockets, two of which were for grenades and one for a pistol. In winter this uniform was covered by a heavy cotton flight overall which was discarded on landing. There was no personal equipment, all ammunition and food being carried in the pockets. Quite naturally the naval airborne troops were not expected to operate for long without logistic support; they were in fact a raiding force who would drop a short distance inland and then make their way back to the beaches.

Like the army the naval parachutists had a type of crash helmet, but by 1944 they were wearing the standard naval steel helmet. They also had special rubber jump boots which reached halfway to the calf, but by 1944 these too had been replaced with standard-issue jungle footwear.

Both army and navy parachutists wore a distinguishing badge on their parade uniform and for security reasons this badge was not worn outside Japan. The army badge was a golden kite, the legendary bird of Japan, with outspread wings. The bird was in gold on a scarlet background and was worn on the right arm just below the shoulder seam. The navy had a circular dark-blue patch with two crossed parachutes superimposed on an anchor and a cherry blossom above. This decoration was in red embroidery, and the patch was worn on the left shoulder.

In summary, Japanese parachute uniforms started with plenty of originality but soon were brought into line with the standard field uniform and equipment. This was not peculiar to Japan alone.

Russia

In Soviet Russia there seems to have been little alteration in the equipment and dress of the parachutists for many years. It is

Tashkent 1941: Russian trainees fitting parachutes. The helmet and loose overall is almost unchanged today. (*Imperial War Museum*)

difficult to be sure of fine detail when dealing with Russian airborne troops as only very general information is released about them and press photographs are not usually explicit. Since the 1930s all parachutists have worn a one-piece overall outer garment. This is usually black or very dark green, and is worn over whatever clothing is suitable to the climate. The actual uniform is the same as is worn by other infantry, though this is only a parade or barracks dress. The overall is the dress for parachuting, and it seems likely that it is worn throughout the operations undertaken after landing. Recent magazine photographs show parachutists moving through woods and attacking objectives, and all are wearing the one-piece overall.

The pre-war Soviet parachutist carried no personal equipment. On his head was a cloth or leather flying helmet. Jumpmasters wore goggles, probably because they were required to expose themselves in the slipstream throughout the run-in over the drop zone. The cloth helmet has survived today and it is worn both in the air and on the ground after the jump. The steel helmet is never seen in operational pictures and appears not to be worn by airborne troops. There is also still some mystery about the personal equipment of the Soviet airborne soldier. There is no sign of kitbags or weapons containers being carried on the man. Some photographs show a small container being carried into the aircraft, but so far it is not possible to determine exactly how it is brought to the ground. Press photos of parachutists in the air show no signs of bags hanging below the men, and it must be assumed that apart from his personal weapon, the Soviet parachutist jumps lightly loaded and collects his kit from containers dropped separately. To some extent this theory is borne out by pictures of parachutists taking part in ground exercises when they apparently carry little or no equipment on their backs. However, some have been seen with small haversacks of a different pattern from the normal infantry one.

Boots are almost certainly the standard Soviet military pattern, as are the gloves. The entire ensemble shows up most clearly in photographs of May Day parades when truck loads of parachutists roll through Red Square, the men sitting in rows in open lorries wearing their overalls, cloth helmets, and parachutes. On these occasions they carry their weapons prominently, but there is rarely any sign of equipment or ammunition pouches.

8 Post-War Developments

World War II ended on a cautious high note for airborne forces. Cautious because, although the theory had been seen to be sound, the execution had on occasions fallen short of expectations. There was also the uncomfortable feeling that the whole idea was far more expensive than it looked from the outside. Soldiers were not alone in this feeling, and in an article to the British *Army Quarterly* published in July 1948 Air Chief Marshal Sir John Slessor had this to say:

> I do not pretend to have attempted even a rough estimate of the total cost of airborne forces by the end of the war – of transport aircraft, gliders, training aircraft, crews, RAF ground personnel both in first line and training units, of the airborne units of the Army and their mass of specialised equipment and stores. But I believe it to be no exaggeration to say that, compared to that cost, the much publicized 500 million spent on the atomic bomb would not appear a very formidable figure. Whether all that expenditure of national effort here and in America was justified by results or whether equivalent or greater dividends might not have resulted from its investment on other kinds of force, I would not care to have to say.

Cut-backs

But Air Marshal Slessor did say it really – he felt it was not worth it. Others on both sides of the Atlantic agreed with him, and the immediate result was a cut-back in the size and scope of the airborne forces in both armies. This was less worrying for the Americans than for the British because the Americans had the aircraft, and the British had not. But the basic trouble was an attitude of mind. The glittering successes of the German airborne in 1940 and 1941 had been tarnished somewhat by the Allied losses at Arnhem and Nijmegen; commanding officers had resented their best men volunteering for airborne duties, and the airmen resented being transport hauliers for parachutists. Came peace and the regular forces could get back to 'proper soldiering' or its air force equivalent, and forget about the 'funnies'. The British cut down to one regular division and one reserve division, but then, with the disappearance of the US Air Force, the air lift was reduced to little more than a battalion group, and it remained as small as that for several years. To some extent this was justified by the tactical thinking of the day, which recognised that by and large the smaller operations had succeeded better than the larger ones in the recent war, and airborne warfare was seen to yield a better return if used on a relatively small scale in support of some other complimentary land operation, rather than by trying to do it all from the air. One can pick holes in this argument now but in 1945 the operations in Corregidor, Bruneval, the Markham Valley, and the rescue of Mussolini could be produced as proof of the idea – and it must be admitted that it gave some comfort to those who were responsible for reducing the force. The fact that they were later proved wrong is just one of the hazards of the strategic prophet.

The British sent their parachute force to the Middle East to act as an infantry force, and later to Germany in the same role. The Americans left theirs at forts in the continental USA where they tried to keep up their expertise under a continual pressure from the manpower planners. Two divisions remained in being, the 82nd and the 11th (later to become the 101st) but strength declined in the units. Training however continued at a brisk rate, and several big exercises were held in 1947 and 1948 in which the landing of a large World War II type force was practised, including the use of an impressive number of gliders for flying in the heavy equipment. During this time the British were doing little by comparison although they caught up in the last years of the 1940s when the Parachute Brigade returned to the United Kingdom from its service abroad. By now the regular force was reduced to one brigade of three battalions and supporting arms, with a division in reserve. It was used as a strategic reserve force, and in 1951 went to Cyprus at short notice because of the unsettled state of affairs in the Middle East at that time. The brigade left in May

A mass drop by men of the 82nd Airborne Division from C-119 transport. (*Keystone*)

Hauling up a dropping beam into the bomb-bay of a Halifax IX. The crated jeep and 6-pounder gun will fall away from the beam when released, and the beam stays in the plane. Note the parachutes in trays and the crash pans under the wheels.

1951, and the last large airborne exercise it had done had been 'Exercise Oil King' in the August of 1950, when one lift of C-47s was mustered and a battalion was put down on a drop zone in Norfolk in the impressively short time of three minutes – though without heavy equipment. There was a little parachuting in the winter of 1950/1, but for many of the brigade there was no jumping until the battalions were transferred to the Suez Canal Zone in the autumn of 1951. By now the Handley-Page Hastings had entered RAF service and most of the troops had to do a short conversion course.

The Hastings

A large four-engined aeroplane, this was capable of carrying thirty parachutists and dropping them in two simultaneous sticks through port and starboard doors. It was the first double-door aircraft in British service. It had a good range and a reasonable lift, but it was unsuited to airborne use because it had a two-wheeled undercarriage and so rested its tail on the ground. Loading was through side doors and there was no question of dropping heavy equipment from inside – instead the obsolete dropping beam from the wartime Halifax was in service with jeeps and guns crated up and fitted with crash pans.

167

The Valetta

At the same time the wartime C-47 or Dakota was relegated to resupply duties and the Vickers Valetta introduced as its replacement. The Valetta was a military version of a civil airliner which had been designed to catch the 'DC-3' market among the post-war airlines. In this it had a limited success, but as a military transport it had little to offer that the Dakota did not already have. The only possible advantage was in range and a slight gain in speed; otherwise the Valetta carried just about the same load rather less conveniently than its predecessor. Its main drawback was the fact that the wing main spar ran across the passenger compartment about two-thirds of the way up, and this spar was a formidable obstacle to a man carrying a kitbag – so much so in fact that kitbag-carriers had to be in the front part of the stick. The spar was about 18in high and 1ft across, forming a solid box running across the floor and if soldiers' curses have any potency the designer must have been a dead man from the day that the first plane entered service. With these two barely suitable aircraft the brigade trained hard.

The Fairchild

In the USA the two airborne divisions were better fitted. In 1944 the design was started on a transport aeroplane for the invasion of Japan and although it was not built in time for that unnecessary operation, its construction was continued and in 1946 the Fairchild C-82 or 'Flying Boxcar' appeared. It was a twin-boom twin-engined high-wing transport not unlike the Gotha 244 in general outline, though differing in many vital respects, and it possessed the ability to be loaded through the rear doors, and to drop heavy loads through them. Guns and jeeps could be parachuted over the door sill at the back and quite large bundled loads could be run along an overhead monorail to be parachuted through the same exit. There were drawbacks to the C-82 it is true – the radius of action was short and this limited the scope of operations that could be mounted with it – and the ability to land and take off from rough strips was not all that could be desired – but it was a step in the right direction and by 1949 the US airborne had ceased to use gliders at all for bringing in heavy equipments and were parachuting them from the Boxcar. By the time the Korean War came the airborne were ready for it.

The Korean War

It was not long after the start of that war that an airborne force was dropped. The 187th Regimental Combat Team was parachuted on to two drop zones north of Pyongyang on 22 October 1950; 2,900 men were dropped from 120 aircraft, 80 C-119s and 40 C-47s. The C-119 was an improved C-82 with more power and a better lift, they carried forty-six paratroopers each and in addition had ammunition and supply bundles hanging on their internal monorails so that they had to fly with their rear doors removed. The C-47s carried ammunition and supplies only. All the aircraft returned for a second and third lift and the C-119s parachuted twelve 105mm howitzers, four 90mm guns, four 3/4 ton trucks, 39 jeeps, 38 trailers, and 584 tons of ammunition and supplies on to the two drop zones. It was an impressive display of the advances that had been made since the last air assault five years before and it was the first time that artillery and large vehicles had been parachuted in quantity. In the next year, March 1951, the 187th again dropped behind the enemy, this time taking 3,300 men, carried in ninety-five aircraft with the same quantity of heavy equipment and supplies. Curiously they used C-46s instead of C-47s to augment the C-119s. It was the last big operation airborne drop, for no subsequent one has matched it for size although there have been many exercises and demonstrations which have been as big or even bigger.

Indo-China

In the same part of the world – Asia – the French were fighting to hold on to the remnants of their south-east Asian empire. From 1946 onwards they were involved in a desperate struggle with the Viet Minh in Indo-China. In this country they found airborne operations to be the answer to strategic mobility and between 1946 and 1954 they mounted 156 separate parachute operations, seldom larger than a company in size and frequently smaller. They used a mixture of Junker 52s seques-

French and Vietnamese parachutists in a C-47 in 1951. Their equipment is a curious mixture of American and British. (*Keystone*)

trated from the Germans, backed up by a few C-47s and later some C-119s. In the last stages their own Nord Atlas 2501 appeared to replace the more elderly machines. The Nord Atlas was a French design, very similar in outline to the C-82. It proved to be an excellent medium-range and medium-payload troop-carrier which the French built in quantity and sold to several NATO countries as well as Israel. It carried forty-five troops at 250mph for a radius of action of just over 900 miles, and this distance could be increased if the load was reduced. Take-off and landing runs were reasonably short and the construction and equipment were kept as simple as possible. It was a substantial step forward from the Dakota and a marked improvement on the then current British aircraft which the British airborne forces were forced to use.

Airborne forces in modern warfare

Korea was a sharp reminder to the Western nations that airborne forces still had a role to play in modern warfare and it caused a hurried stocktaking among those who had let their standards slip.

The Beverley

The British realised with a jerk that they had no aircraft capable of launching their airborne division into anything like the two operations so successfully undertaken by the 187th, and some hurried searching among the existing designs in the British aircraft industry produced the dusty blueprints of a machine known as the General Electric Freighter – later to be called the Beverley. This machine was designed in 1944 for the expected airborne operations in northern Germany in 1945. It had a massive lift over a short distance, a relatively slow flying speed, and virtually no capability to carry troops or freight over any strategic distance. It was a short-range tactical freighter, pure and simple. By 1954 it was well out of date, but with no other design on hand it was decided to accept the limitations inherent in a ten-year-old idea and try to reduce them as far as possible by modifications. The alternative was to wait several years more while a fresh design was drawn up, tested and tried.

In many ways the Beverley was an amazing machine. One eminent American aerodynamicist used to entertain his after-dinner guests by proving mathematically that it was impossible for it to fly, but fly it did for the best part of twelve years all over the world, without ever actually being used in a full-scale war. On the short hauls it could carry two medium platforms or ninety-eight men in the troop-carrying role – rather less as paratroopers. Thirty of these were in the enormous tail boom, which was larger than the entire fuselage of the C-47. When dropping heavy equipment on platforms the crews of those loads travelled in the boom and jumped after their loads were dropped. Their exit was through a hole in the floor, just as in the Halifax, although more comfortable because there was plenty of room to stand up and approach it. Originally it had been hoped that three sticks of parachutists could jump simultaneously from two doors in the fuselage and the boom, but tests showed that the danger of entanglement was extreme and it was never done. The result was that when there was a full load of parachutists the ones in the boom had to climb down into the belly and join on to the fuselage sticks to exit as two long lines through the doors. This spread everyone out on the drop zone and meant a long walk to the rallying point so that it was not looked upon with favour by the troops.

Nevertheless, the Beverley gave the British their first aircraft with rear-opening doors and it meant that heavy loads could be carried easily and dropped by parachute from inside the fuselage. This was a substantial step forward but it came too late for the next airborne operation which the world was to witness at Suez in 1956.

Suez

On the first night of the campaign the Israelis dropped a battalion of 400 men from C-47s onto the Mitla Pass in the Sinai. They dropped without heavy weapons and their aircraft had to fly back two hours later to deliver these. They then parachuted 106mm recoilless anti-tank guns, jeeps, mortars and ammunition; the jeeps and 106s being dropped from Nord Atlas planes borrowed from the French. Six days later the British and French struck at Suez.

In the early morning of 5 November two waves of troop-carrying aircraft headed south from Cyprus to Port Said. The first wave consisted of fourteen Hastings and eighteen Valettas of the RAF carrying the 3rd Parachute Battalion Group. The Valettas carried troops only, the Hastings lifted a mixture of troops and heavy equipment. The drop, onto El Gamil airfield to the west of Port Said started at 7.15 am and was over within a few minutes. This was the largest operational jump undertaken by British airborne forces since the end of World War II and through no fault of those taking part it was probably also the most troublesome and embarrassing. The root cause of the difficulties was aircraft, or rather the lack of them. It is no exaggeration to say that the 3rd Battalion went to action in Port Said in almost exactly the same way as it had done at Arnhem twelve years before. The exceptions were the absence firstly of C-47 Dakotas and secondly of gliders. In retrospect the gliders at least might have had their uses. Suez was a completely parachute operation for the airborne force, and it came at a most awkward time. The Valetta and Hastings were both obsolete, but their replacement had yet to be built – this was to be the Beverley, but at the time of Suez only one existed. The only way to carry heavy equipment was underneath the Hastings using the same dropping gear and techniques as with the Halifax in 1944, and this was so restricting and expensive that the operational stocks of dropping gear and associated equipment were being allowed to waste out against the time when the Beverley would appear to change everything. Suez came when there were hardly any left and the mounting of the heavy drop from Cyprus was not easy. The shortage of dropping beams was so severe that one had to be taken out of an unofficial museum at the Air Transport Development Centre and hurriedly flown to Cyprus to make up the number. The 106mm recoilless gun had just been adopted as the anti-tank gun for airborne forces, but there was no satisfactory way of dropping it from an exterior cradle. After much hurried testing and improvisation, a method was found which allowed the gun to be parachuted without damage; but this was hardly the way to prepare for a battle.

The men wore uniform and equipment almost identical with what had been worn at Arnhem and apart from the few 106mm recoilless guns they had the same weapons too. Even the jeeps were the same type although there were many Land-Rovers on Cyprus; but the dropping beams on the Hastings only accepted the jeep and they had to be taken for the initial jump. The troops used the then current X-type parachute and, as has been noted in the chapter on parachutes, they jumped without reserves. Dropping height was quite low, just over 500ft seems to be the generally accepted estimate, and there were the usual minor troubles with the heavy drop, resulting in damage to some of the vehicles. In all other respects the drop was near enough a perfect demonstration run, the result in no small part of excellent flying by the pilots.

The French landed on a tiny drop zone only 500 by 200yd with buildings all round it. To decrease the chances of drifting off it they jumped from 300ft, lower than any other operation except that of the 503rd on to Noemfoor Island. Indeed, the French had considered using helicopters but ruled them out because of the number of Egyptian anti-aircraft guns in the surrounding area. They felt, correctly as it turned out, that helicopters would be too vulnerable as they flew in and out, whereas the transport aircraft had only to make one pass and would be in the danger area for a much shorter time. Nowadays with the experience of Vietnam to go by, the decision might well be different, but air assaults by helicopter were very much in their infancy in 1956.

Later developments

The real lesson which came out of Korea, and later Algeria, was the extent to which the helicopter had changed the tactical mobility of the troops on the battlefield and from 1955 onwards the story of airborne forces becomes more and more involved with helicopter operations; however parachute forces were by no means neglected although for some countries, particularly Britain, it was often difficult to decide where to spend the slender military budget in order to obtain the best operational effect and value. The Beverley was pushed ahead and came into service in the late 1950s at almost the same time as its more modern counterpart in the USA. The American plane was the C-130, known in British service as the Hercules, and in many ways its specification closely matched that of the Beverley. Both were four-engined high-wing monoplanes with rear-opening doors to their cargo compartments. Both carried about seventy paratroops or two heavy drop platforms; both could land and take off from short unprepared strips; both were tough and versatile. But the similarities ended there. The C-130 was a strategic as well as a tactical transport with a radius of action of 1,500 miles carrying a combat load, and it could fly the major part of that distance at high altitude with its cargo or troop compartment pressurized, coming down to tree-top height for the final approach, and opening the rear clam-shell doors to drop out a platform or some similar load. Alternatively paratroopers could jump from side doors. It was a modern parachute-assault aircraft in every respect and alongside it the Beverley looked like an antique.

At this same period, the late 1950s, similar advanced types of troop-carrying aircraft appeared from designers around the world. One which was sold well to many small independent countries in need of a parachute force was the Canadian De Havilland Caribou, a twin-engined tail-loading machine with a lift of four tons or some twenty-six paratroops. The Caribou was remarkably robust and versatile with an astonishingly

Present-day Soviet parachute troops lined up behind their An-12 transports. Although this is a military jump, not one man is carrying a weapon or a container.

short landing and take-off run. Even the Russians followed the general trend with their four-engined Antonov An-12 appearing in the later 1950s as a copy of, or rival to, the C-130. The two are very similar except that the Antonov has a gun turret in the tail, which is not a fashionable idea with western countries, nor, one would think, is it of any great utility in these days of high-speed flying. Like the C-130 the Antonov has rear doors which can be opened in flight, and it can drop heavy equipment on platforms or skid-boards. The full load of paratroops is just short of sixty, and they jump from two doors, one either side of the after end of the fuselage.

The appearance of the Antonov coincided with a resurgence in the importance of the Russian airborne army and from 1957 onwards a feature of the Russian military parades and manoeuvres has been the display of airborne forces and their equipment. The speed with which the lost ground has been made up has been impressive. The skills of dropping heavy loads and organising the complicated apparatus of an airborne assault appear to have been mastered and even special equipment has been produced. The foremost of these is the ASU-57, or airborne self-propelled assault gun. This is a 57mm anti-tank gun mounted on a light armoured chassis, which was first seen in 1957 at a May Day parade. It weighs 5·5 tons, has a

The enormous An-22 unloading an anti-aircraft missile on its tracked vehicle at a Moscow air display.

crew of three, a top speed on roads of 34mph, good cross-country performance, and sufficient armour to protect the crew from small arms' fire. Thirty of them are in the anti-tank battalion of the airborne division. There is no exact equivalent in the West, and in 1957 there was nothing which even approached it, a fact which made its appearance even more important to Western observers. Since this exciting start in 1957 the Soviet airborne forces have been featured many times in military magazines and films. There is no doubt that much importance is attached to the idea of parachute assaults, and this despite the fact that the Soviets have been among the leaders in the use of helicopters on the battlefield – plainly they feel that there is still an important job for the parachute-delivered force in a modern war, a tenet which is not always echoed on this side of the Iron Curtain.

By the late 1960s the Soviet airborne army had seven VDV divisions (VDV – *Vozdushno Desantinye Vovska*) each of 7,500 men and two Special Service brigades. The airlift for this force has been maintained at a strength sufficient to carry three of the division at one time, although not all the aircraft are necessarily the latest type. In addition to the Antonov An-12s there are rather more elderly Ilyushin Il-18s, Antonov An-24s (which equate to the American C-123) and Ilyushin Il-14s. Nevertheless the potential is considerable, and powerful supporting forces can be flown in to back up the parachute troops once an air strip has been either captured or cleared. The An-12s can air-land 85mm self-propelled guns for anti-tank defence, together with field artillery and light tanks. These forces are kept at a high state of readiness, and although their past actions in World War II could hardly be described as successful, there is every reason to suppose that were they to be committed to operations today things would be very different.

In land mobility, no country seems to have made any great advances for its airborne forces. Throughout the 1950s and early 1960s there was continuous research by private manufacturers to build a satisfactory lightweight vehicle for parachute troops, despite the fact that it had been well established in the war that once on the ground parachutists became the same as normal infantry and so had the same requirements from their transport. Most of the private venture ideas started from the wrong end, that is they were built down to a size and weight which meant that they lacked the carrying capacity and power for a battlefield vehicle. The exception was the US Army's Mule, a small flat platform with four wheels and an engine underneath the loading space. It carried about half a ton, weighed roughly the same unladen, and was meant as an ammunition carrier or as a means of moving a weapon, but all was done at little more than walking pace. Indeed the steering wheel was capable of folding so that the driver could walk alongside when carrying the maximum load and still control the vehicle.

The other designs, and there were many of them, tried to carry men as well as ammunition, and in some cases the motive power was a motor-cycle engine. Few had adequate ground clearance or strength, although they looked most attractive in their manufacturers' brochures. There is really no substitute for sheer strength and horsepower in both military and support vehicles; in these respects the parachutists have advanced only a short way in the thirty years or so since World War II ended. In the Western world today there is still no satisfactory

(*over page*) A Land-Rover rigged on a stressed platform, ready for loading into the plane. (*Airborne Forces Museum, Aldershot*)

light tank for airborne forces, no adequate artillery support that can be parachuted with the initial force, and no specialised self-propelled anti-tank artillery to protect the force from armoured attacks. The main means of movement is still the jeep – or its counterpart – and the soldier's foot.

But there have been advances and changes in parachutes since 1945. The British – with some reluctance – changed over to an improved X-type in the early 1960s and called the new design the PX. It has a larger canopy with a deeper rounded shape to it, so that when in flight it has a more pronounced shape than the X-type. The rate of descent is slower and the stability greatly improved, but it is otherwise an X-type. The US Army made much the same sort of change a few years earlier and replaced the T-7 with the T-10. This was rather more of a radical move than the British one for the T-10 uses the canopy-last opening technique. It is very little different from the PX, except in minor details of manufacture, and its size and flight characteristics are the same.

These two parachutes are used by a large proportion of the airborne armies of the Western world to-day, only the French preferring to manufacture their own designs, but these follow the same general pattern as the PX and the T-10.

One other post-war innovation which has expanded the military use of parachutists is the use of the free-fall technique. Originally a fair ground stunt in which the parachutist thrilled the crowd by dropping without opening his parachute until as close to the ground as he dared, free-falling is now a highly developed and skilful art which requires much careful training and continuous practice. Large groups of men cannot be delivered in this way, but for inserting small bodies of raiders, saboteurs, scouts and long-distance patrols there are some circumstances in which the free-fall drop has no equal. The delivery plane can fly high and fast and it need never make any obvious change in its flight pattern that could be interpreted as a run in to a drop zone; the parachutists bundle out as it flies straight and level at any height up to 15,000 or 20,000ft. They

An experimental 100ft diameter cargo parachute dwarfing a man beside it. Such large single canopies are usually too difficult to handle when on the ground, and so are not practical. (*Keystone*)

A Soviet demonstration jump in 1955. The design of the canopy shows very clearly, as do the small pockets around the rim which assist the canopy to open. (*Keystone*)

then drop like stones, undetected by radar, to open their canopies at less than 2,000ft above the ground and land in one group – still without the enemy radar knowing of their existence. Each man can carry 60lb of weapons and equipment, but naturally no heavier equipment of any sort can be dropped with them. They are a lightly armed and equipped special force who cannot be expected to fight a normal infantry action. The development of this highly specialised form of parachuting has been greatly helped by the spread of civilian 'skydiving' and it is no accident that in most countries the national experts are from the military forces. The parachutes used for free-falling are somewhat different from those used by the static-line jumper. The free-fall canopy is much more highly developed and nowadays it may not even be circular; there are some canopies which descend slowly but glide almost like actual aeroplanes and these are often rectangular or triangular in shape. Dropping with one of these parachutes is indeed very much like flying a low-speed flying machine: they move through the air at speeds of up to 15mph and can be turned, manoeuvred and flown with considerable precision. The circular canopies have holes and slots cut out of them to let the air form jets and give a positive drift to the jumper so that he can pick his landing place and drive for it even though the wind may not be helping him. At night the men often wear small lights so that they can see each other and remain in a group until landing. The standard of individual skill required for this sort of parachuting is considerable, and it requires continuous and demanding practice.

Various ways have been tried for steering free-fallers onto their appointed landing area but few have been so dramatic as the one used by the Russians at the start of the resurgence of their airborne forces in 1956. At the Tushino Air Show that year, a dozen or so parachutists landed on the aerodrome in a demonstration jump using a revolutionary new technique. Each man jumped from about 12,000ft and immediately opened a small square parachute roughly 6ft square. This stabilized his fall without slowing him down or allowing him to drift off the target. When at a normal opening height for the main canopy, the small parachute was released and it then acted as a static line for the main parachute and pulled it out of its container and deployed it smoothly before floating away on its own. The group all landed in a very small area of the aerodrome, without having to do any steering or manoeuvring in free-fall at all. Although there have been variations on this theme from time to time, and Captain Kittinger used a version of it in his famous world-record jump from a balloon at 102,200ft, it does not seem to have been adopted as a regular method of dropping.

Airborne warfare is just over thirty years old. It started as a means of achieving short-range strategic mobility and surprise. The limitations of aircraft and equipment quickly turned this into a concept of a rapid air assault followed by static defence which had to continue until conventional ground forces could link up and free the defenders. Once the parachute force was committed it became very nearly totally inflexible and if anything went wrong with the link-up operation, the airborne force was in desperate straights. This is the essence of a parachute operation, it is a strictly one-way movement and the

Germans summed it up neatly in their 'Song of the Paratroops' two lines of which are:

> 'Into the 'planes, into the 'planes!
> Comrades, there is no going back!'

Indeed there is no going back once the troops have jumped; parachutes do not go upwards. Although the air assault and seizure concept still holds, the range of the operation has greatly extended with modern aircraft: there is now scarcely any place in the world which cannot be reached by parachute troops. Yet once on the ground they are still largely immobile. In time the helicopter or some derivation from it will be developed so as to have the same range as the present fixed-wing

French parachutists in Indo-China, June 1951. Helmet and gunbelt are WWII American. Patterned uniform, berets and thick-soled jump boots are entirely French. (*Caravane*, Paris.)

Retour à HANOI (fin juin 1951)

transport – when it does appear, the whole concept of airborne warfare will be changed, for once troops can be put down and taken up again over strategic distances they possess enormous flexibility and would pose an even bigger threat than they do today.

However, until such time, and until such a machine is perfected and put into service, the parachute soldier using his proven advantages of long-range penetration, speed into action and above all, surprise – will continue as an effective and necessary arm in the ranks of any first-line army.

Bibliography

(In alphabetical order of titles)

Airborne Forces. T. B. H. Otway. London: the War Office, 1951
Airborne to Battle. M. A. J. Tugwell. London: William Kimber, 1971
Aircraft of the Third Reich. William Green. London: Macdonald, 1972
Airpower and Russian Partisan Warfare. General der Flieger Karl Drum. New York: Arno Press, 1965
Airspeed Aircraft Since 1931. H. A. Taylor. London: Putnam, 1968
Die Armeen der Ostblockstaaten. Friedrich Wiener. Munich: J. F. Lehmans Verlag, 1968
The Balloonatics. Alan Morris. London: Jarrolds, 1970
A Bridge Too Far. Cornelius Ryan. London: Hamish Hamilton, 1974
British and American Tanks of World War II. Chamberlain and Ellis. New York: Arco Publishing Co Inc, 1969
British Parachute Forces 1940–1945. Howard P. Davies. New York: Arco Publishing Co Inc, 1974
By Air to Battle. Charles MacDonald. London: Macdonald, 1970
The Fall of Eben Emael. James E. Mrazek. New York: Hale, 1972
The Fortunes of War. Andrew A. Rooney. New York: Little, Brown and Co, 1959
German Airborne Troops. Roger Edwards. London: Macdonald and Janes, 1974
German Airforce Airlift Operations. Generalmajor Fritz Morzik. New York: Arno Press, 1965
The Guns 1939–1945. I. V. Hogg. London: Ballantine, 1971
History of the 1st Airborne Battle Group. Public Information Office, 1st Airborne Battle Group, 1958
Infantry Weapons of World War II. J. S. Weeks. London: Ballantine, 1971
Japanese Aircraft of the Pacific War. R. J. Francillon. London: Putnam, 1970
Lion With Blue Wings. Ronald Seth. London: Gollancz, 1955
Military Small Arms of the Twentieth Century. I. V. Hogg and J. S. Weeks. London: Arms and Armour Press, 1973
Prelude to Glory. Maurice Newnham. London: Sampson Low, 1952
The Red Devils. G. G. Norton. London: Leo Cooper, 1970
The Russian Airforce in the Eyes of the German Commanders. Generallieutenant Walter Schwabedissen. New York: Arno Press, 1966
Soviet Transport Aircraft Since 1945. John Stroud. London: Putnam, 1968
The Special Air Service. Philip Warner. London: William Kimber, 1959
The Stuka Story. Heinz Nowarra. New York: John W. Caler, 1964
The Tenth. R. Brammall. Norwich: Eastgate Publications, 1964
War and Peace in the Space Age. Lt-General James M. Gavin. New York: Harper, 1963
Wings of Pegasus. G. Chatterton. London: Macdonald, 1955

SECONDARY SOURCES

The Armstrong Whitworth Whitley. P. J. R. Moyes. Windsor: Profile
   Publications Ltd, 1970
The Douglas Dakota. A. Pearcy. Windsor: Profile Publications Ltd, 1969
The Douglas DC-3. A. Pearcy. Windsor: Profile Publications Ltd, 1969
Ordnance Technical Intelligence Reports, 1943–1946. US Army
Training Manuals. US and British armies
Various magazines, including *The Aeroplane, Flight, Aeroplane Spotter, Air
   Enthusiast* and others.

Acknowledgments

Inevitably I have drawn on the experience and knowledge of others in
preparing the text; one cannot write a book such as this entirely on one's
own. The number of persons who have helped me is far larger than I can
mention here and I must ask those who do not see their names to forgive the
omission. To them all I shall always be grateful.

I am particularly indebted to Major G. G. Norton and Mr Fitch of the
Airborne Forces Museum in Aldershot. Both were unfailing in their
assistance and encouragement and were at all times willing to delve into their
excellent records to clear some obscure point, or to examine an actual
specimen among the large and comprehensive collection that that museum
enjoys.

I have also drawn freely upon the generosity of the US Army Museum at the
Infantry Center, Fort Benning, the Airborne Museum at Fort Bragg, and the
Quartermaster Corps Museum at Fort Lee.

Invaluable reminiscences of the Suez Campaign of 1956 were provided by
my old friend Major Bill Hancock, who was a forward air controller in that
operation.

The staff of the Photographic Library of the Imperial War Museum were, as
always, knowledgeable and helpful. So too were the ladies who run the
Pentagon Photographic Library.

John Blake made the drawings, in record time, while convalescing from an
operation. His encyclopedic memory of matters military and aeronautical,
together with his wit and humour, were a constant joy.

My publishers encouraged me throughout and I have been enormously
impressed by their patience and confidence. May their firm prosper!

Mrs Walker and Mrs Ponting typed the manuscript, deciphering my random
jottings and complicated instructions. The typescript was read and corrected
for me by Lt Colonel Rick Stokes, Royal Canadian Artillery and Brigadier
Maurice Tugwell, late of the Parachute Regiment.

187

Index

191